U.S.-MEXICAN WAR

WAR

Revised Edition

U.S.-MEXICAN WAR

Revised Edition

BRONWYN MILLS

JOHN S. BOWMAN
general editor

CHELSEA HOUSE
PUBLISHERS
An imprint of Infobase Publishing

U.S.-Mexican War, Revised Edition

Copyright © 2010, 2003, 1992 by Bronwyn Mills
Maps copyright © 2010, 2003 by Facts On File

Chelsea House
132 West 31st Street
New York NY 10001

Library of Congress Cataloging-in-Publication Data
Mills, Bronwyn.
U.S.-Mexican War / by Bronwyn Mills ; John Bowman, general editor.—Rev. ed.
p. cm. — (America at war)
Includes bibliographical references and index.
Summary: Chronicles the causes and events of the Mexican War, from Mexico's
struggle for recognition as an independent country to the war's end in 1848.
ISBN 978-0-8160-8195-0 (hc : alk. paper) 1. Mexican War, 1846–1848—Juvenile
literature. [1. Mexican War, 1846–1848.] I. Bowman, John Stewart, 1931–
II. Title. III. Series.
E404.M55 2010
973.6'2—dc22   2009046082

Text design by Erika K. Arroyo
Cover design by Takeshi Takahashi
Composition by Hermitage Publishing Services
Cover printed by Bang Printing, Brainerd, Minn.
Book printed and bound by Bang Printing, Brainerd, Minn.
Date printed: September 2010
Printed in the United States of America

10 9 8 7 6 5 4 3 2 1

This book is printed on acid-free paper.

Notes on Photos

Many of the illustrations and photographs used in this book are old, historical images. The quality of the prints is not always up to modern standards, as in some cases the originals are from glass negatives or are damaged. The content of the illustrations, however, made their inclusion important despite problems in reproduction.

Contents

Preface

With the end of the U.S.-Mexican War in 1848, the United States had grown to include nearly all the land now referred to as the 48 contiguous United States. Not all the territories within that vast land had achieved full statehood, and before the U.S.-Mexican War even began, the northern and southern states were engaged in a feud. Ostensibly it was over the issue of statehood, but underneath that lay a fundamental disagreement: Which newly acquired states and territories would be slave and which would be free? The argument persisted right through to the next war.

This book is about that "in-between" time, that "in-between" war, the U.S.-Mexican War, which gained so much territory, set the tone for relations between the United States and Mexico for years to come, and contributed far more than is generally acknowledged to the next major conflict—the sad and difficult Civil War. It might also be said that this is the "in-between" war in another sense—a war that has fallen in between the cracks of the history of the United States as it is usually presented and studied. It is worth taking a moment to consider some of the reasons why this "minor" 19th-century war still has much to say to people in the 21st century.

In its time, the U.S.-Mexican War sparked the enthusiasm of many expansionist-minded U.S. citizens as well as the ire of their more boundary-respecting compatriots. But since this book was first published in 1992, the U.S.-Mexican War has remained a relatively unpublicized war—although no less controversial than it always was. A recent addition (2007) to the study of this war that does address the controversy is Joseph Wheelan's *Invading Mexico: America's Continental Dream and the Mexican War, 1846–1848*. A serious study, Wheelan's book refers to the "dubious pretext" that caused Taylor's army to cross the Rio Grande—the claim that American blood had been spilled on U.S. soil—and also argues that the U.S.-Mexican War was the first modern war. Wheelan also argues that it was an ideological conflict that attempted to decide if the United States should be an urban manufacturing state or a nation of small farmers.

However, more often than not, a visit to a major bookstore produces few books about it, let alone any new ones. A knowledgeable bookseller may mention Richard Bruce Winders's *Mr. Polk's Army: The American Military Experience in the Mexican War* (1997) and direct a persistent reader to the military history subsection of the history shelves. Winders's work is scrupulously researched: He draws from diaries, journals, reminiscences—in short, from primary materials, to paint a detailed and fascinating picture of the day-to-day life of soldiers in the 1846–48 army. But the book does not concern itself with dissenting commentary, and some readers may find that it glosses over the distasteful issues of that time. Indeed, Winders's recognition of controversy seems to be limited to describing the different responses men had to the leadership styles of Zachary Taylor versus "Old Fuss and Feathers," Gen. Winfield Scott. All in all, Winders concludes that the U.S. soldiers emerged from that war with a sense of shared experience. Indeed, the book's importance lies in putting the everyday life of soldiers in some kind of real world context.

So Far from God: The U.S. War with Mexico 1846–1848 (2000), by John S. D. Eisenhower, originally published in 1989, has been rereleased in paperback. The book takes its title from a comment attributed to Gen. Porfirio Díaz, dictator president of Mexico from 1877 to 1911 ("Poor Mexico! So far from God and so close to the United States.") Historian Robert V. Remini, reviewing it in the *Washington Post*, praised the book as a splendid narrative of "this 'dirty little war'"—to use the phrase coined at the time (and since applied to all manner of wars). In his work, Eisenhower looks at the pros and cons of the war and the rationale for U.S. entrance. He, too, has been meticulous in his research.

A book that takes a different approach is *Manifest Destiny and Empire: American Antebellum Expansionism* (1998), a collection of essays covering the subject of Manifest Destiny leading up to the eve of the war with Mexico in 1846. Robert Walter Johannsen, chief editor, has written an able introduction to the book as well as the first chapter, devoted to explaining Manifest Destiny itself. Johannsen has published books on the war with Mexico and on that period. Indeed, his fascination, as is suggested by the title of his earlier work, *To the Halls of the Montezumas: The Mexican War in the American Imagination* (1985), is not with fact so much as with fiction. In that earlier book, he examines North American fantasies about the war and its peoples.

There are other books that might be cited, but the fact is that the U.S.-Mexican War has not claimed many "buffs." And it is hard not to conclude that the reason for this silence is that the rationale for the war was, and continues to be, questioned. Although in narratives of the war, flamboyant characters such as Gen. Zachary Taylor, Cmdr. Robert Stockton, Col. Alexander Doniphan, and the Mexican general Antonio López de Santa Anna are writ large, one issue argued since the beginning of the war seems to have pushed them into the shadows of history: Did U.S. forces actually trespass into Mexican territory, and thus provoke the war, or not? Many scholars suggest that the United States was the aggressor. The *Washington Post*'s reference to the "dirty little war," in fact, recalls the doubt surrounding U.S. involvement, tarnishing the glories of that war versus the clearer glories that are celebrated by enthusiasts of the Revolutionary War, Civil War, World War I, and World War II. It is hard to imagine, for example, the U.S.-Mexican War ever inspiring the kind of individuals who annually gather in full uniform and gear to "reenact" the battles of the Revolutionary War or Civil War. It might also be pointed out that no major American novelists or poets of that era (or since, for that matter) have been moved to write a work inspired by that war.

Another measure of Americans' interest in a given war has long been the numbers and kinds of movies that have been inspired by that war. Probably, most Americans could not think of a single movie based on the U.S.-Mexican War (although there would be some based on the fall of the Alamo). There is one relatively recent (1998) if not widely known film, however, directed by Lance Hool and starring Tom Berenger, *One Man's Hero*, which focuses on the San Patricio Brigade, the Irish Catholic regiment that fought with the Mexicans during the war. With the exception of a few floggings and anti-Catholic remarks to set the tone, the film, though useful, does not show the viewer the full picture in terms of the reasons why these men were so dissatisfied that they actually abandoned the U.S. Army for the enemy camp. It carefully avoids any reference to the atrocities committed by Yankee troops against the Roman Catholic missions and against the

Mexican civilians, yet these have been documented by historians and profoundly shocked these Irish (Catholic) troops. Mexicans today still regard the men of the San Patricio Brigade as heroes.

The degree to which the war itself was either unpopular or supported in the United States of the time also continues to be a subject worthy of discussion. At least one historian has said that it was as unpopular back then as the Vietnam War was in the 1960s and 1970s. Indeed, as this volume clearly recounts, young Abraham Lincoln challenged "President Polk's War" from the floor of the House. It is often forgotten, too, or conveniently overlooked, that Henry David Thoreau's world-famous text *Civil Disobedience* grew out of his own challenge to the war by refusing to pay his taxes. And as indicated above, Roman Catholic Irish recruits, sickened by the treatment of Mexican civilians and the desecration of the Mexicans' Roman Catholic churches, challenged the war by deserting to the other side.

Above all, the issue that continues to remain bothersome, both as a "fact" of history and as a precedent for U.S. policy, is the question of whether the United States deliberately provoked the conflict by crossing into Mexican territory. After President James Polk sent troops into Texas in anticipation of military action, no one was surprised when, soon after, on May 11, 1846, he addressed Congress asking for a declaration of war: "[Mexican forces] after a long-continued series of menaces have at last invaded our territory and shed the blood of our fellow-citizens on our own soil." But a young lieutenant in one of the first U.S. Army units assigned to the Louisiana border with Texas would later write: "We were sent to provoke a fight, but it was essential that Mexico should commence it." This was Ulysses S. Grant writing his memoirs 40 years later.

In fact, although Polk argued before Congress that the United States had been unduly pressed by Mexico, the move across the river into Mexican territory had been planned months before. Grant's attitude, at least as expressed later, could hardly have been more vehement: "I do not think there ever was a more wicked war than that waged by the United States in Mexico. I thought so at the time, when I was a youngster only I had not moral courage enough to resign."

In his memoirs, Grant would also have something important to say about a related issue that continues to make this war relevant in any discussion of U.S. policies in more recent decades: the manner in which the U.S. Congress "declares" war.

It was very doubtful whether Congress would declare war; but if Mexico should attack our troops, the Executive could announce, "Whereas, war exists by the acts of, etc." and prosecute the contest with vigor. Once initiated there were but few public men who would have the courage to oppose it. Experience proves the man who obstructs a war in which his nation is engaged, no matter whether right or wrong, occupies a not enviable place in life or history. Better for him, individually, to advocate "war pestilence, and famine," than to act as obstructionist to a war already begun.

Clearly, then, the war with Mexico should not be dismissed as an irrelevant little war. The war, for example, brought a series of military firsts for the relatively new United States: the first major war fought on foreign soil, the first major amphibious landing (at Veracruz), and the first implementation of a major strategic campaign—Scott's extraordinary march on Mexico's capital. It also provided a model of a war in which sheer might prevailed, for U.S. firepower certainly remained superior throughout the conflict. The lesson learned in this war—that by employing overwhelming hardware, the risk to lives and limbs of U.S. personnel is kept to a minimum—is one that the U.S. military would apply in wars to follow.

Another of the most interesting developments in the study of this war is a new move on the part of U.S. and Mexican scholars to look at the conflict jointly. In 1989, a modest volume was published, entitled *The View from Chapultepec: Mexican Writers on the Mexican-American War.* Translated and edited by U.S. scholar Cecil Robinson, the book was little noticed, although one of its aims was to offer North American readers the opportunity to inform themselves of other perspectives at the time. In his introduction, Robinson provides an excellent analysis of the several controversies around the declaration of war and takes a closer look at the difficulties that beset a newly independent and much weakened Mexico in conducting its own defense. This book signals one of the first steps of an effort on both sides of the Rio Grande to examine the war as scholars rather than combatants.

Subsequently, in 1998, PBS produced a documentary, *The U.S.-Mexican War (1846–1848),* and launched a Web site to accompany it (http://www.pbs.org/kera/usmexicanwar). Featuring leading scholars and authorities from both sides of the Rio Grande, this project is remarkable in its balance and lack of rancor and serves as a valuable resource for serious students of the war. The History Channel Presents series' 2008 release of a TV/DVD film on the subject, *The Mexican-American War,* also refers to that war as one of the most controversial in U.S. history and goes to admirable lengths to present the conflict from the perspective of both nations involved.

Online, however, the attempts at a balanced perspective seem more difficult to access. *Wikipedia,* the "open source" encyclopedia, attempts to summarize the key facts about the war and does attempt some objectivity regarding its controversial nature. Indeed, our volume is cited on their webpage: http://en.wikipedia.org/wiki/Mexican-American_War. Still, many so-called informational sites, such as About.com, seem to skim over any analysis of the war's causes, proceeding directly to its chronology and descriptions of its battles and those who led them. History Guy is one exception—http://www.historyguy.com/Mexican-American_War.html—but the difficulty of determining which are and are not reliable sites, endemic to the use of the Web in general, is particularly troublesome in the case of this neglected conflict.

Indeed, as the collaboration of Mexican and U.S. historians now demonstrates, the issue is no longer whether the U.S. involvement in the war against Mexico was justified.

More recent depictions of the war, in short, have acknowledged its controversial nature and include that in their discussion of present-day Mexico and Mexican-U.S. relations. Clearly, the loss of its northern territories was an unqualified economic disaster for Mexico, but it is useful to know that Mexican "underdevelopment" set in as early as 1810, grew during the decade of the war for independence from Spain, and continued right through the war with the United States. Another nail in the coffin of Mexican progress, the defeat in this war retarded change that was very slow to come in the first place.

And these are not just remote academic issues. To the extent that the loss of its territories north of the Rio Grande was a major blow to the economy of Mexico, the reverberations from the U.S.-Mexican War continue to this day—and the impact continues to be felt in both countries. Most notable, poor Mexicans have continued to cross U.S. borders in search of a better life than they can often find in their own homeland. In fact, to the casual observer, it may seem that the loss of northern Mexican territories made little difference, as the contiguous border has been consistently porous. The North American Free Trade

Agreement (NAFTA), in effect since 1994, gives every sign of still further breaking down that border.

The permeability of the border has long had other consequences besides the movement of populations, but the 2007 inauguration of the wall between the United States and Mexico has generated some difficult discussion within and without both countries. In 2009, construction was halted as representatives of both nations struggled to find an honorable and diplomatic solution to the problems of emigration and immigration and, especially, the illegal drug trade. The latter alone is a staggering problem. As the 21st century proceeds, the majority of the illegal cocaine arriving in the United States continues to come via Mexico, as does most of the heroin made in Colombia, as does Mexican black tar heroin, a significant amount of street methamphetamine (or "speed"), and a large tonnage of the annual marijuana crop.

While policing the 2,000-mile-long border has not been made any easier by the recent construction of the wall, the continued drug traffic has made the law enforcement even more difficult. Legal exporting and importing of Mexican products has suffered as a result of all the energy and resources expended fighting illegal trade. Further, when the United States reorganized its drug enforcement agency in 1973, forming the Drug Enforcement Administration (DEA), the almost immediate effort to internationalize drug enforcement raised issues of national sovereignty. Understanding the history of the U.S.-Mexican War of the 1840s should help in understanding why this might be a very sensitive issue for Mexicans. In Mexico, however, there has been increased mutual cooperation in enforcement along the border, in spite of the fact that the lucrative trade has naturally created corruption, risk, and unfortunate loss of life.

For descendants of the original Mexicans in the Southwest, still another legal issue persists. The dilemma of how to honor the old Spanish land grants is very much alive, especially in New Mexico. In May 2001, the U.S. Government Accounting Office (GAO) extended the deadline for reviewing an Exposure Draft, a report regarding land grants that were issued by Spain and later by the Republic of Mexico and were to be honored by the United States under the Treaty of Guadalupe-Hidalgo. The comments of Nuevo Mexicanos (Mexicans who hold these land grants in present-day New Mexico) were requested at that time, and the outcome as of late 2002 is still not known. (The contents of the Exposure Draft can be viewed on www.gao.gov/guadalupe.)

The issue is further complicated by the fact that several parcels among the disputed lands are now public areas under protection as environmental treasures. Thus, 19th-century and 21st-century issues collide in rather surprising ways.

A history of a war fought in a distant past and a foreign land inevitably employs some unfamiliar words: *dragoon,* for example, which at that time had a particular meaning, or words in Spanish, such as *gringo.* To help readers keep track of these and many other relevant terms, the book contains a valuable glossary. There are many maps and plans prepared especially for this book, and among the many more appealing elements of the book are the boxes, or sidebars, small essays or articles that deal in some depth with topics that supplement the main text.

In addition to these features, this revised edition has several new ones. It has numerous color illustrations that should enhance the attractiveness of the book. It has a new sidebar titled "A Just War?" specifically designed to elicit debate on the pros and cons of this admittedly still controversial conflict. There is a completely new chapter, "Weapons and Tactics," isolating those very topics while placing them in the context of the war on the ground. Finally, the recommended reading and Web sites have been updated.

All these features and the well-established text make this revised edition an even more valuable and engaging account of this all-too-often neglected episode in the history of the United States. And at a time when Americans of Mexican descent are becoming an increasingly larger proportion of the population of the United States, it becomes more important than ever to recognize and understand this war's role in U.S.-Mexican relations.

CROSSING THE BOUNDARY

It was the afternoon of March 28, 1846. At the head of his troops, Brig. Gen. Zachary Taylor of the U.S. Army, a rather short, thickset man with a drooping mustache, bent forward and shifted his weight in his saddle by pushing on his saddlehorn. He wore a common soldier's light blue overalls and an old brown coat. It was early spring in southeastern Texas or, depending on how one looked at it, northern Mexico. The weather was certainly warm enough to make a person sweat, and perspiration glued the general's clothing firmly to his back.

Taylor kept his soldiers on the move. Mules and horse dragged big guns along on creaking iron wagon wheels. To the clink of spurs and metal bits in their harnesses, uniformed horsemen guided their animals along the banks of the wide, shallow river. It was the Rio Grande, Spanish for "Great River." It flowed along what Texans had not long ago regarded as the southern boundary of the independent Republic of Texas and divided it from its former mother country, Mexico. Only three months ago, Texas had become the 28th state of the Union, and now the U.S. Army was here on the alert.

What had happened that the United States was preparing to confront Mexico with armed force? The full story of the two nations' differences was complex and went back many years. But the showdown began in 1835, when North American settlers in Texas started the battle for independence from Mexico. After some six months of fighting, the Texan-Americans had won and declared the Republic of Texas. In spite of this defeat, Mexico would not formally recognize Texas as an independent republic. From the very outset, it was known that many of the men who fought for Texas's independence really wanted to join the United States. And although the land had always belonged to Mexico,

1

President James K. Polk (1795–1849), whose actions precipitated the war with Mexico *(Library of Congress)*

the Mexican government suspected that sooner or later the United States would interfere and try to make Texas a state. Indeed, at the signing of the Adams-Onís Treaty of 1819—when Spain ceded Florida to the United States—a condition the United States agreed to was to relinquish any claims to Texas. Independent Mexico inherited Spain's agreement as still binding, and Mexico threatened to declare war if the United States ever tried to claim Texas.

Ten years passed, and friction increased between the United States and Mexico. After the failure of an attempt to get the U.S. Senate to adopt a treaty annexing Texas as a state, President John Tyler resorted to a vaguely unconstitutional tactic and on March 1, 1845, three days before he was to leave office, signed a joint resolution of the U.S. Congress to admit Texas as a state. On March 4, Tyler was succeeded as president by James Polk, who had actively campaigned on the platform of annexing Texas. In his inaugural speech, Polk even declared that Texas's annexation was none of Mexico's business. On March 31, 1845, Mexico broke off diplomatic relations with the United States to express its displeasure.

Texas had not yet joined the Union, but President Polk acted as though it were already a state. At the end of May, he asked Gen. Zachary Taylor to take a detachment of troops from New Orleans to Texas to protect Texas against Mexican "invasion." On June 11, 1845, Polk was even more specific. He ordered General Taylor to take a shipload of troops and move them "on or near the Rio Grande." On July 31, 1845, on his way south, Taylor stopped. He positioned his forces at Corpus Christi, the last North American settlement in Texas. They made camp on the Nueces River, the river that the Mexican government reluctantly regarded as the boundary between the Republic of Texas and Mexico. But it was still many miles north of the Rio Grande.

Maj. Gen. Zachary Taylor (1784–1850), whose victories in the war with Mexico gained him the presidency *(Library of Congress)*

By October of 1845, 4,000 troops, nearly half of the entire U.S. Army, waited in Corpus Christi. To the southwest, between the Nueces and the Rio Grande, stretched an area claimed by both Texas and Mexico, though it was settled entirely by Mexicans. Texas had never controlled it. Even Mexicans who were willing to recognize Texas's independence disputed a Texas boundary as far south as the Rio Grande.

Already suspicious, some American leaders argued that even entering the disputed territory between the Nueces and the Rio Grande would be an act of war on the part of the United States. In fact, former president Anson Jones of the Republic of Texas accused the United States of trying to "annex a war" when it tried to annex Texas. From this point of view, when Taylor advanced it meant war for sure.

Diplomacy failed to win peace between the two nations. On December 29, 1845, Texas officially joined the Union. On January 13, 1846, Polk ordered Taylor to enter the territory between the Nueces and the Rio Grande. He was to take his troops all the way to the Texas side of that great river. At the outset, Mexican general Francisco Mejías sent a formal note to Taylor protesting his advance. But the soldiers marched on. They arrived on March 28, 1846, that hot spring day when a perspiring General Taylor positioned all 4,000 troops along the banks of the Rio Grande.

This is a view of General Taylor's camp at Corpus Christi, Texas, where his army of some 4,000 troops spent the last months of 1845 before moving down to the Rio Grande in territory claimed by Mexico. *(Library of Congress)*

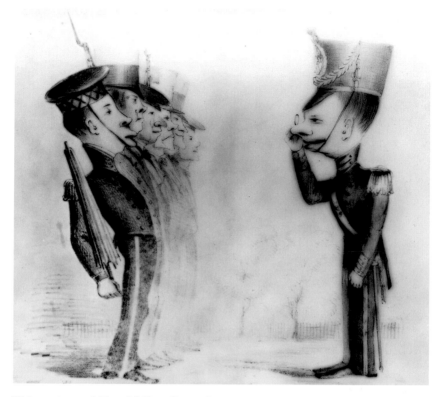

This cartoon of May 1846 reflects the public's opinion of the poor caliber of volunteer troops for the U.S.-Mexican War. *(Library of Congress)*

Taylor's men gathered across the river from the little town of Matamoros, not more than 25 miles from the spot where the Rio Grande emptied into the Gulf of Mexico. There they constructed a fort that looked out over the river. In spite of another note of protest from local Mexican authorities, they established a base of supplies at Point Isabel, right where the Rio Grande emptied into the Gulf of Mexico. Taylor's army consisted of one regiment of dragoons (heavily armed mounted soldiers), five regiments of infantry, and four batteries of field artillery. This, Taylor said, "seemed fully adequate to meet any crisis which might arise."

While he waited, however, Taylor had his hands full. To add even more anxiety to the wait—a situation in which tension mounted but no battles began—the recruits were getting restless. A plague of poor discipline and just plain brutality spread, and it included more and more outrageous acts against civilians, especially in the form of repeated desecration of the Mexicans' Catholic churches and attacks on Spanish-speaking worshipers. This latter practice so enraged Irish Catholic volunteers in the U.S. Army that some began to leave its service in Matamoros and join the Mexicans. As early as April 6, Taylor reported that four such "deserters of conscience" had been drowned and that pickets (men standing watch) had shot two others trying to join the other side by swimming the Rio Grande. Taylor saw these departures as the result of "efforts . . . to entice our men to desert." Later in the month, 30 more swam the river in protest of the brutalities of their fellow recruits, and they formed the nucleus of a unit in the Mexican army known as the "San Patricio Brigade," composed of U.S. deserters in the Mexican army. These soldiers would fight by the side of the Mexicans until the end of the war, when they were captured by the U.S. forces in Mexico City. Declared traitors, their faces were branded with a *D* (for deserter) and they were hanged on the gallows.

Such violent developments still lay in the future, but flogging and other corporal punishments were used from the outset in Taylor's

One Man's Hero, a 1999 movie, starred Tom Berenger as John Reilly, an Irish-American who deserts the U.S. Army because of its mistreatment of his fellow Roman Catholic Irish and becomes a leader of the San Patricio Brigade. A mix of fact and fiction, it is the only Hollywood movie devoted to this war (not to be confused with films about Mexico's earlier war with Texas). *(Orion Pictures/Photofest)*

camp for various infractions. That also angered the troops. Soon the officers were showing discontent. At least one brigadier commander was arrested and relieved of his duties for "neglect of duty and being 'tight.'" One of Taylor's officers, Gen. Worth, stormed back to the United States because he and Taylor got into a disagreement.

Then, on April 10, Col. Trueman Cross left camp by himself and did not return. A search party led by Lt. Theodric Porter, went out to look for him. On April 19, soldiers straggling in reported a fight in a rainstorm in which Porter and others were killed. The atmosphere around Matamoros was like gunpowder waiting for a match.

On April 11, the Mexican troops stationed at Matamoros had welcomed a new commander and 2,000 more soldiers. With a ceremony that included a 21-gun salute, Gen. Pedro de Ampudia replaced Gen. Francisco Mejías. Then, just minutes after his arrival, Ampudia sent a messenger across the river demanding that Taylor immediately break camp and retire to his own territory behind the Nueces. Ampudia demanded action within 24 hours, "otherwise arms and arms alone will decide the question."

His orders, Taylor replied, did not permit retreat. Taylor stayed put. At the same time, he ordered a naval blockade of the mouth of the Rio Grande. Another exchange of notes followed. If the U.S. claim was legitimate and the Rio Grande was the boundary between Mexico and the United States, then Taylor had just ordered the blockade of an international boundary. If the Nueces was the boundary, a blockade was definitely a hostile act against Mexico.

Ampudia's term was short. On April 24, Gen. Mariano Arista replaced him. The third Mexican commander at Matamoros in a month, Arista was a tall, freckle-faced man with sandy hair and red whiskers who had lived several years in Cincinnati. He was fluent in English. Later, he became one of Mexico's presidents.

Arista took charge quickly and immediately sent Taylor a note stating, "I . . . consider hostilities commenced, and shall prosecute them." Taylor replied that he had done nothing that "could possibly be interpreted as hostility," and he added that whoever made the first move would have to take that responsibility. That same day, Arista sent Gen. Anastasio Torrejón and 1,600 cavalry across the river above Matamoros.

When he heard of the crossing that evening, Taylor sent out a group of 63 dragoons to scout out the situation. The patrol of dragoons, led by Capt. Seth Thornton, spent the entire evening hunting for Torrejón.

On April 26, news of Thornton's search party came early. Taylor's bugler sounded reveille. In the middle of the bustle and grumble of soldiers waking up and getting a morning meal, a man on horseback galloped up to Taylor's headquarters. He was the Mexican guide who had accompanied Thornton's party, and he brought bad news. The day before, Thornton and his dragoons entered a Mexican settlement. At a ranch called Carrecitos, they were trapped in a corral by Torrejón and his soldiers. The Mexican force killed 11 dragoons outright, others were wounded, and almost all were captured. That afternoon, Torrejón sent a wounded dragoon back in a cart with a polite note explaining that the Mexican troops were without a hospital to care for the wounded properly, but the other officers were being held as prisoners of war. The wounded man confirmed these reports.

Out came the U.S. artillery on its iron wheels. Cavalrymen and dragoons saddled their horses, the animals whinnying at the smell of leather and sweat and excitement all around them. Saber blades were sharpened, gun barrels cleaned, knives burnished. With a blast of the bugle, Taylor's troops assembled. That day, April 26, 1846, General Taylor sent a message to Washington that "hostilities may now be considered as commenced."

"BLOOD ON AMERICAN SOIL!"

From the moment General Taylor ordered the U.S. Navy to blockade the mouth of the Rio Grande on April 12, 1846, anyone looking closely at events in that region must have been anxious. Already, it could be argued, Taylor's armed presence below the Nueces River, technically Mexican territory, was an invasion; moreover, by international law, blocking the port of a sovereign nation was an act of war. Thus no observer was surprised when, on April 23, three days before Taylor announced that hostilities had begun, Mexico's President Paredes condemned the United States for its aggression and declared that Mexico would begin a "defensive war" against the U.S.

In 1846, before telephones and other modern means of communication, and before the newly invented telegraph reached such remote regions as this, news inevitably took a long time to go from Texas to Washington. As late as May 9, 1846, President Polk confided to his diary that he and his cabinet agreed—just one hostile act on Mexico's part and the United States would go to war. At 6 P.M., General R. Jones, the adjutant general of the army, handed the president General Taylor's dispatch regarding the outbreak of hostilities near Matamoros.

At 7:00, Polk called together his cabinet. War it was, and that very evening, at 10:00, Polk went to his desk to prepare his war message to be read to Congress the following day:

> After repeated menaces, Mexico has passed the boundary of the United States, has invaded our territory and shed American blood upon the American soil. . . .

Although he went on to say that "the cup of forbearance had been exhausted," Polk was hardly weary. Rather, he was reportedly

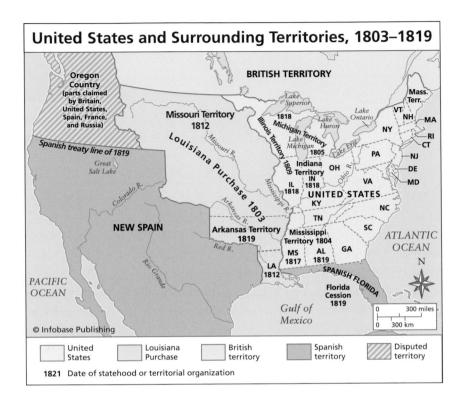

United States and Surrounding Territories, 1803–1819

Oregon Country (parts claimed by Britain, United States, Spain, France, and Russia)

BRITISH TERRITORY

Spanish treaty line of 1819

Great Salt Lake

Missouri Territory 1812

Louisiana Purchase 1803

Lake Superior

Lake Huron

Lake Michigan

Lake Ontario

Lake Erie

1818

Michigan Territory 1805

Illinois Territory 1809

Missouri R.

Mississippi R.

Indiana Territory

IN 1818

IL 1818

Mass. Terr.

VT

NH MA

NY

RI CT

PA NJ

OH DE

VA MD

UNITED STATES

KY

NC

TN

SC

NEW SPAIN

Colorado R.

Arkansas R.

Red R.

Arkansas Territory 1819

Mississippi Territory 1804

MS 1817

AL 1819

GA

ATLANTIC OCEAN

N

Rio Grande

LA 1812

SPANISH FLORIDA

PACIFIC OCEAN

Florida Cession 1819

Gulf of Mexico

0   300 miles

0   300 km

© Infobase Publishing

United States | Louisiana Purchase | British territory | Spanish territory | Disputed territory

1821 Date of statehood or territorial organization

delighted. Nor did news of war surprise Congress. The long history of the two countries' conflict over this territory made it almost inevitable.

One argument made to justify a war against Mexico was that Mexico had fallen far behind in paying the reparations due American citizens because of damage to their property and harm to their persons during Mexico's frequent and violent revolutions. Yet it was public knowledge that, in 1842, several U.S. states had refused to repay debts to foreign creditors and now the U.S. debt totaled $200,000,000, or roughly 10 times more than what Mexico owed Washington. Therefore, Polk surprised many Americans when he listed Mexican debt as a reason for the war.

A more realistic "debt" behind the war was the one that many Americans felt they owed to their own history. Since the time of the Revolution, Americans had dreamed of a United States that stretched across the entire continent. By the 1840s the drive for westward expansion had become a national passion. As James Polk's predecessor, President Tyler, wrote in 1842 to his minister to Mexico, Waddy Thompson: "The acquisition of [Mexico's] California is a thing uppermost in the public mind." Tyler went on, "Do you think it is possible to bring it about?" It seems fair to conclude that the war with Mexico was primarily fired up by U.S. expansionism—that is, the idea that U.S. settlers should possess more and more of the North American continent.

Quite aside from the fact that as soon as Europeans set foot in the New World they stepped on land belonging to someone else—Native Americans—the United States still had to share North America with other nations. A look at a map of North America in 1800 shows that U.S. territory was primarily limited to the 13 original states along the East Coast—Massachusetts, New Hampshire, Rhode Island, Connecticut, New York, New Jersey, Pennsylvania, Delaware, Maryland, Virginia, North Carolina, South Carolina, and Georgia—plus a few new states, Vermont, Kentucky, and Tennessee. It also included the Northwest Territory, an area won through the Revolution and consisting of the present states of Ohio, Indiana, Illinois, Michigan, Wisconsin, and part of Minnesota. The United States also claimed the "Western," or Mississippi Territory.

Nueva España, or New Spain, as the Spanish called their vast holdings in North America, included all territory between the Mississippi River and the Pacific Ocean—Canada to New Orleans, and from present-day Texas to down into Mexico. Spain also owned what it called the Floridas. Roughly speaking, the Florida panhandle, extending to the Mississippi and including New Orleans, was Western Florida; the peninsula was Eastern Florida. Nueva España did not include the Oregon Territory, which was held by Britain.

As noted, many people in the United States had wanted New Spain and the Floridas at least since Thomas Jefferson expressed that thought in 1786. Then, in November 1801, eight months after he became president, Jefferson heard that Spain had made a secret treaty with France to give France all of Louisiana (roughly the large area between the Mississippi and the Rockies extending from Canada to New Orleans). The United States opposed the transfer of North American territory to another European power. Jefferson urged U.S. ownership of the Floridas (Eastern and Western) and, especially, New Orleans, and let France know that the United States was willing to buy the territory.

Several diplomatic exchanges later, in 1803, the United States bought the entire Louisiana territory from France for 60 million francs—roughly $15 million. The Louisiana Purchase, as the sale was called, gave the United States a huge territory, rich with resources,

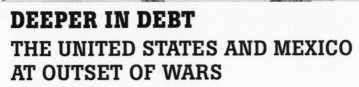

DEEPER IN DEBT
THE UNITED STATES AND MEXICO AT OUTSET OF WARS

Generally, Protestant Europe's colonies in the Americas produced wealth—sugar, tobacco, cotton—while Spain simply plundered, leaving little behind. Further, as Europe focused on the French Revolution and 25 years of related wars, a newly independent United States prospered while Mexico was drained: $5 billion in Mexican silver and gold went to Europe between 1760 and 1809. Mexican silver financed the Napoleonic Wars (1804–15); and yet Britain, the winner, France and Spain, the losers—all went bankrupt. New Spain was then reorganized to refill European coffers, not colonial ones.

In 1827, Mexico defaulted on two major British loans and lost its credit. French invasion of Veracruz in 1838 coerced Mexican president Anastasio Bustamante into guaranteeing France 600,000 pesos from Mexican customs. In 1843, already indebted to Washington, Mexico defaulted on $3 million worth of payments of damages to U.S. citizens harmed by Mexican wars and confiscation. Demands for payment of this debt would become one of the factors that justified the war against Mexico in the eyes of some in the United States.

nearly doubling the area of the nation. As part of a small tail of land surrounding the Mississippi delta, the purchase also included the coveted city, New Orleans. That meant a clear trade route for U.S. farmers down the Mississippi and into the city of New Orleans.

This enlarged United States remained the same until the War of 1812, fought against the British. At that time, Spain was Britain's ally, and, when the United States declared war against Britain, it thought nothing of annexing all of Spanish-claimed Western Florida. After the War of 1812 was over, skirmishes over Eastern Florida and crossings into Mexico's Texas (from the New Orleans side) occurred on a regular basis.

On January 8, 1815, a U.S. cavalry commander nicknamed "Old Hickory"—the future U.S. president Andrew Jackson—gained notoriety by beating the British at New Orleans with an army of scrubby volunteers in hunting shirts. He continued to make headlines into the 1830s, in part as an advocate of "Indian Removal" who personally fought to drive Native Americans out of their lands. U.S. pioneers, prospectors, and trappers swarmed in to take their place.

In 1818, Jackson began the first of the so-called Seminole Wars in Eastern Florida. He went after the runaway slaves and displaced Native Americans who survived by crossing over into the U.S. South and raiding farmers' stores. He burned the villages of the Florida Indians, the Seminole. He seized Spanish forts. Finally, Spain was forced to agree to the Florida Purchase of 1819. By this agreement—the Adams-Onís Treaty—the United States bought Florida for $5 million and surrendered any claims to Texas. Signed on February 22, 1819, it set the southwestern boundary of the United States with Mexico at the Sabine River, the river that divides present-day western Louisiana from Texas. It kept the boundaries between Nueva España and the United States, effectively confirming that Texas, the present-day Southwest, and California belonged to Spain.

In 1821, Mexican citizens won their independence from Spain. In the process of liberating itself, Mexico inherited the agreements signed by Spain, including the Florida Purchase, or as it is also known, the

The U.S. forces' victory over the British at the Battle of New Orleans on January 8, 1815, gave support to those who felt the United States had a right to adjacent territory held by Spain and then Mexico. *(Library of Congress)*

In a cartoon designed to denigrate Zachary Taylor in his campaign for the presidency in 1848, he is depicted on horseback *(right)* as commander of the U.S. forces in the Second Seminole War, (1835–42), encouraging U.S. troops' brutal treatment of the Seminole Indians. *(Library of Congress)*

Transcontinental Treaty. New Spain simply changed its name and became the Mexican Empire.

But as Mexico entered its first tumultuous decades as an independent nation (including those years of the U.S.-Mexican War), the United States was establishing its own hemispheric foreign policy. In response to continued European interest in the hemisphere, on December 2, 1823, President James Monroe announced one of the most significant initiatives in the history of U.S. foreign policy: the Monroe Doctrine. It said that the United States would keep out of the internal affairs of European states—but European nations must keep out of all the Americas, South and Central as well as North. The Western Hemisphere was to embody the principles of freedom unlike the European nations that, Monroe claimed, were "laboring to become the domicile of despotism."

Thanks to the efforts of expansionists such as Andrew Jackson, by the 1820s a rich agricultural paradise dubbed the "Cotton Kingdom" emerged: most of Florida and Alabama, Tennessee, Georgia, Mississippi, Kentucky, and South and North Carolina. This Cotton Kingdom

introduced yet another dimension to the debate about the Mexican War, for slavery sustained the region's productivity and wealth. If regarded as an evil that would at some future time need to be removed by someone, North and South could agree about slavery. However, abolitionists—those calling for the freeing of the slaves—wanted abolition of slavery at once, not in some comfortably faraway future. Plantation owners and those profiting from the unpaid labor of slaves, on the other hand, thought of each state as an independent entity that had the right to decide what happened within its borders (the doctrine of "states' rights"). The more slave states and territories there were, proslavery factions thought, the better chance such an economic system had of surviving.

Thus, as each new state entered the Union, there was a fight in the House and in the Senate: Which would those states choose to be, slave or free? And with the addition of the "Cotton Kingdom," the numbers of slave states and proslavery legislators increased. It began to look as though Southerners would become the majority in the U.S. Congress, and the cry for land—and new slave states—grew louder and louder.

Furthermore, although the United States officially avoided involvement in Latin American affairs, including those of Mexico, it unofficially sold weapons and sent secret agents into their neighbors' land. These agents brought propaganda and copies of the U.S. Constitution to push independence from Spain. (Not surprisingly, Mexico imitated the U.S. Constitution when it framed its own in 1824.)

On January 17, 1821, a Connecticut Yankee named Moses Austin had persuaded Spanish-ruled Mexico to open its gates officially to Anglos—the name commonly given to the English-speaking settlers in Spanish-speaking territories. Settlers simply had to agree to become Mexican citizens and adopt Roman Catholicism. Almost immediately, Mexico became independent, but it assured the settlers that it would honor U.S. settlers' agreements with Spain. Moses Austin died soon thereafter. His scholarly son Stephen took up the cause. Stephen Austin's efforts were responsible for two things: Mexican willingness to allow further settlement, and the tremendous wave of settlement by Anglos between 1825 and 1830. But the two conditions originally set forth—becoming Mexican citizens and adopting Roman Catholicism—were met on an offhand, individual basis.

As the newly independent Mexican government began to organize itself, President John Quincy Adams, who had previously negotiated the Florida Purchase of 1819 with Spain (the one that renounced U.S. claims on Texas) sent Joel R. Poinsett to Mexico City as its ambassador. But Poinsett was given a secret agenda, to offer to buy Texas from the Mexican government. He was to argue that one result of getting rid of the upper part of Mexico was that it would put Mexico's capital nearer the center of the country. This absurd argument—and the offer—was rejected, and to many Mexicans and foreigners in Mexico, Poinsett's name became a synonym for ruthlessness. Constantly involved in various diplomatic intrigues, Poinsett was finally recalled, in 1829, by Adams's successor, Andrew Jackson. (An amateur botanist, he brought back a plant he was developing, and it soon was named after him—the poinsettia.)

Between 1825 and 1830, many *estadounidenses* ("Unitedstaters") came to Texas without authorization, bringing their slaves into Mexican territory, often in defiance of Mexican law, which abolished slavery in 1829. Mexico was simply not strong enough to force total abolition of slavery on its U.S. colonists. Nor, in many cases, could it persuade them to pay taxes to the Mexican government. As the Mexican government began to realize the unruliness of its English-speaking colonists, it tried to close its borders to U.S. settlers, but by 1832, Anglos in Texas outnumbered Mexicans 24,700 to 3,400.

The presence of the colonists was a source of friction between the United States and Mexico. As time went on, they quarreled more and

General Antonio López de Santa Anna (1794– 1876) *(Library of Congress)*

more over Texas. The conflict came to a turning point in 1834, shortly after Antonio López de Santa Anna successfully overturned the military government of Anastasio Bustamante in Mexico City. This was but one of a constant series of overturnings of the Mexican government that would leave it weak when it came to fight the United States. This instability came about because there were two opposing groups competing to control Mexico: the *federalistas* and the centrists. The situation was further complicated by another faction, the monarchists, who wanted a king installed and some of whom even advocated rejoining Spain.

Essentially, the *federalistas* wanted a Mexico consisting of a loose organization of independently governed states. The centrists wanted a strong centralized government. Centrists (Santa Anna was one) paid more attention to the affairs of the faraway northern Mexican states such as Texas and California; Federalists, though very patriotic, left these states to manage their own affairs, even sometimes their own defense.

Not surprisingly, Anglo-Texans favored federalism, as they wanted to form a state with little interference from the central regime. During this period of Mexican upheaval, Anglo-Texans agitated for more freedom to govern themselves. They even petitioned Santa Anna to set up Texas as an independent Mexican state. That request was rejected, and its bearer, Stephen Austin, was jailed in Mexico until July 1835. When Austin was released, he returned to Texas and set about working for a completely independent Texas.

In exchange for land at four cents an acre, U.S. "volunteers" (especially from the Cotton Kingdom) came pouring over the border to fight the Mexicans. Hostilities between Santa Anna and a force led by Austin broke out on October 2, 1835. Five hundred Anglo-Texans crossed the Guadalupe River, just north of San Antonio, and forced Santa Anna's army into that town. With Stephen Austin in command, the rebels then took San Antonio. Still, in November 1835, Anglo-Texans called a convention to decide if they wanted to pledge loyalty to the liberal (Federalist) Mexican Constitution of 1824 or go independent: The vote was 33 to 15 in favor of the Constitution. Then these men offered to join any Mexican state that wanted to resist the centrist moves of Santa Anna, and they elected one Samuel Houston as major general of the provisional government of the still Mexican state of Texas.

By February 23, 1836, Santa Anna's forces besieged 188 Anglo-Texan mercenaries who had taken refuge in the Alamo, a mission in San Antonio. Toward the end of the siege, on March 2, 1836, the radical

In taking the Alamo on March 6, 1836, Mexican troops killed most of the defenders and in so doing prompted Americans' desire for revenge that would culminate in the war against Mexico 10 years later. *(Library of Congress)*

Anglo-Texans began framing a "Texan Declaration of Cause for Taking Up Arms"—the Texas declaration of independence. On March 6, Santa Anna finally broke the siege at the Alamo. His troops killed every man in the mission, including the famous Davy Crockett and Jim Bowie, who allegedly invented the bowie knife.

Not all historians agree as to whether any civilians were in the Alamo—some sources say three women, two children, and a young black slave survived; others say more were present. But the Alamo gave the Mexicans a reputation for brutality. It was harder to dispute that reputation when, three weeks later, news came of another disaster for the Anglos—the execution on March 27 of some 330 Anglo soldiers at Goliad, a small town some 60 or more miles southeast of San Antonio.

On April 20, 1836, Santa Anna ordered his forces to make camp near the San Jacinto River (east of modern Houston). Confident after the Alamo and Goliad that the final victory for Mexico was in his grasp, he had decided that the *norteamericanos* would not attack until April 22. Then, on April 21, as the camp lay still in the hush of siesta hour—"Remember the Alamo! Remember Goliad!" shouts broke the silence. Gunshot and cannon roared. Smoke filled the air. With 400 Mexicans killed in the first 15 minutes, this engagement effectively ended Mexican rule of Texas.

Santa Anna fled but as he boarded the ship that would take him to safety, he was dragged from it and put in a prison camp for six months. Sam Houston, it was reported, may have taken pity on the Mexican general because they were both Freemasons: In exchange for his own life, on May 12, 1836, Santa Anna signed a treaty that recognized Texas's independence and its claim to the Rio Grande as its southernmost border. Santa Anna returned to Mexico City, it is said, with his fancy sword worth $7,000 and a wagonful of fighting cocks. Subsequently, Mexico's congress rejected the treaty—insisting that the Sabine River was the boundary.

General Houston, provisional leader of the Texas government, was inaugurated president of the new republic in October 1836. In the two weeks following victory at San Jacinto on April 21, 1836, the provisional constitution that on March 2 had been drawn up, along with the Texas declaration of independence, was ratified. One article, included since March, made Texas's position very clear: Slaves were legal property, and a master was assured perpetual rights over them. If Texas were to come into the Union, then, it would enter as a slave state.

Although what it owed the United States was comparatively small, by 1838 Mexico was lagging further and further behind in its debt payments to several countries. It was so much in debt to France that the French finally took the matter into their own hands and in April blockaded the seaport of Veracruz. With reinforcements, on November 28, 1838, they bombarded the offshore fortress of San Juan de Ulúa. When Mexico declared war on France and ordered all French citizens out of the country, the French commander Charles Baudin raided Veracruz in an unsuccessful search for Santa Anna, who as a hero of the Mexican Revolution inevitably got called to fight invaders.

Santa Anna not only gave his services at that battle; he gave a leg, which was ripped off by a French mortar. He rode out of the city toward

MONARCHISTS, *FEDERALISTAS,* AND LIBERALS
MEXICO'S TANGLED POLITICS

During the 1700s, in the absence of Spanish heirs, the Bourbon dynasty of France extended its rule over Spain and its colonies. Ruling with an iron hand, the Bourbons had the goal of a centralized, monarchical rule. They interrupted the more personal, though paternal, relationships that had existed before them in New Spain and coldly drained these possessions of resources, with no real effort to reinvest anything there. Yet, long after independence, ultraconservative Mexicans, among those who benefited under the old Bourbon rule, yearned nostalgically for a monarch.

After 1821, Mexican political parties drew from the old conservative order that harked back to the middle of the 18th century and from more moderate reform efforts that came along in reaction to Spanish colonial rule. Disappointed with the outcome of 1821, some parties claimed that Spain simply transferred the power of a European upper class to a criollo (native born) upper class. Santa Anna was a part of this criollo caste, and therefore a defender of a centralized government that, by its very existence, excluded country folk and disdained the lower classes, especially those with mixed and pure Indian blood.

Mexico City like a hero, his embalmed leg in a separate wagon. Once in Mexico City, his leg was ceremoniously interred. He went on to dedicate a gilded bronze statue of himself with his hand pointing north. This, he proclaimed, indicated the direction of Texas, the territory he would reclaim.

As Mexico's financial problems worsened, the United States continued to eye Mexican land. The controversy over Texas and the lure of the Far West added glamour to one of the most debated political ideas in U.S. history—Manifest Destiny. Before this idea was even named, it fired the enthusiasm of U.S. immigrants going into Texas to "defend" it from its Mexican owners. It gave sparkle to tales of the new Santa Fe Trail, which opened the West to commerce in silver and merchandise. It fueled U.S. efforts, though unsuccessful, to buy California from Mexico, as Tyler had asked Waddy Thompson to do and as his succes-

By the 1840s, the conservative and liberal parties had multiplied into factions. Conservatives, in general, wanted a centralized bureaucracy like the old colonial Spanish model, a strong army, and a powerful church. From the beginning, the army had been loyalist (monarchist), and thus its members formed the most conservative wing of the Conservative Party. Liberals, meanwhile, in general admired French political theory and North American practice and wanted a secular, decentralized state without the church's drain on the economy.

Among the liberals were those who did not entirely reject their colonial past *(moderados)* and others who most emphatically did *(puros)*. Among the *puros* were the *federalistas,* who in addition to their liberal agenda, wanted to replace the centralized army with local militias. Yet liberals often demonstrated an inbred racism toward indigenous peoples, fearing their potential uprising, and disregarding their communal society for an emphasis on individualism and private property.

At Mexico's defeat in the war with the United States, the conservatives blamed the liberals as conduits for alien ideas and for idealizing the "mongrelized" democracy of the North. Mexico's government veered sharply to the right. This culminated in the later intervention of the French and, to the monarchists' delight, the brief reign of Emperor Maximilian (1863–67).

sors continued to attempt. Thus, in 1845, journalist John L. O'Sullivan belatedly named the concept, already much in evidence, in an article in the *United States Magazine and Democratic Review.* He claimed that it was the United States's "manifest destiny to overspread the continent."

There it was—"Manifest Destiny," the rallying cry for expansionists who believed it was historically inevitable that the United States extend its sovereignty from the Atlantic to the Pacific. Second to that was a belief in "Young America," a term that described an 1840s U.S. attitude about progress that completely ignored the conflict over slavery. The world, according to this idea, was destined to become a republic and a democracy just like the United States.

Manifest Destiny, the hunger for more land for more slaves, a newly independent Texas at the U.S. border—all played a role in opening the door to the U.S.-Mexican conflict. Further, as soon as Texas declared itself independent, Southerners and Democrats began agitating for annexation. Sam Houston's platform had included a bid for joining the States, and all but 61 of 6,000 who voted Houston into office in 1836 favored it. Texas, furthermore, continued to have the problem of fighting off Mexican border raids all during 1842 and 1843. Also, with its paper money worth only 16.6 cents on the U.S. dollar (Mexico's peso, on the other hand, was equivalent in value to the U.S. dollar), Texas existed on a shaky foundation of paper land grants and promises to repay debts. Joining the United States began to look quite attractive.

As far as Mexico was concerned, the United States had encouraged the Texas rebellion with material aid; if the United States were to annex Texas, many Mexicans felt, it meant war. In fact, when Santa Anna returned to Mexico City, he immediately claimed that the treaty he had agreed to on May 12, 1836, had no binding power. As Mexico's president, he continually refused to compromise and he approached the British for their support. Thinking the English support was more secure than it actually was, he stopped payments on the Mexican debt to the United States.

One of the reasons Santa Anna felt he might be able to count on Britain's support in his dispute with the United States was that the United States and Great Britain were engaged in their own dispute over the Oregon Territory. Although Spain and then Mexico had always claimed California from San Diego up to Oregon, Britain had

The Battle of San Jacinto—April 21, 1836 *(Library of Congress)*

This Currier and Ives lithograph, showing Indians looking helplessly over a settlement and railroad, captures the spirit of Manifest Destiny: The United States was destined to expand across the continent. *(Library of Congress)*

long competed with the United States for the Oregon Territory itself (roughly the area of today's Oregon, Washington State, Idaho, parts of Montana and Wyoming, and a block of southwestern Canada). Led by fur traders and missionaries, thousands of Americans had been settling in this vast Oregon Territory since the early 1800s. Signing the Treaty of Joint Occupation of 1827, the United States and Britain agreed to share the region; both countries had made treaties with Russia, which had already given up all claims to territory below latitude 54°40′.

But this was a treaty between national governments, and it did not change the feelings of many Americans. Santa Anna thought he might capitalize on the growing friction between Americans and British over the Oregon Territory. By 1842, enthusiastic "Oregon Conventions" met throughout the American West to demand immediate and exclusive U.S. occupation. In 1844, expansionist Democrats shouted "Fifty-four Forty or Fight," as a campaign slogan (a reference to the territory's northern border), and "All of Oregon or None."

In March 1845, the newly elected Democratic president, James Polk, announced,

> Our title to the country of the Oregon is "clear and unques-
> tionable," and already are our people preparing to perfect that
> title by occupying it with their wives and children.

For one thing, all his supporters expected of him was to take all of Oregon any way he could. Southerners, in particular, wanted to annex free Oregon because it meant an opportunity to annex Texas as a slave state (counterbalancing the entry of a free one).

That December, Polk asked the Senate to cancel its vote for the 1827 Treaty of Joint Occupation, while England sputtered protests. A month later, fearing those U.S. settlers whose idea of law and order was "the Bowie knife, Revolving Pistol and Rifle," London ordered its prosperous Hudson's Bay Company to relocate onto Fort Victoria, a post built on Vancouver Island. Effectively, Britain gave up its claims to at least part of the territory. For the United States, this eliminated the need to fight a war against Britain to obtain Oregon. On June 10, 1846, the U.S. Senate accepted a compromise boundary at the 49° north latitude as the northern boundary of U.S.-owned Oregon Territory. Polk would be free to focus his energies on Mexico. Any hope that Santa Anna had of Britain's possibly even making war against the United States vanished completely with this compromise.

Well before this resolution to the Oregon Territory dispute, however, back in 1844, nearing the end of his presidency, Tyler had appointed John C. Calhoun as secretary of state. As Calhoun took office, former president Andrew Jackson—who still had considerable influence on U.S. policy—urged the United States to take poor, weak, debt-ridden Texas before Britain did. In reality, Mexico was the real threat, as it considered annexation a declaration of war.

Calhoun then negotiated an annexation treaty with Texas, to the horror of northern abolitionists and like-minded opponents. The treaty pledged U.S. protection from Mexico during the transition from independence to statehood. However, on June 8, 1844, the Senate refused to ratify the document, for two reasons: Many senators did not want another slave state in the Union, and many others did not want to risk war with Mexico.

By the end of 1844, the Mexican people had had enough of Santa Anna. On November 2, Gen. Mariano Paredes y Arrillaga, growling at

John Tyler (1790–1862) contributed to advancing a war with Mexico by arbitrarily introducing a resolution to annex Texas in the final days of his presidency. (*Library of Congress*)

Santa Anna's wasteful and corrupt administration, issued a revolutionary manifesto. Commanding the largest unit of the Mexican army in the north, he staged a military coup. Santa Anna sent a message to the U.S. representative dated November 29, 1844, offering (as he had done back in March 1836) to recognize Texas's independence. His own congress condemned him. Angry citizens tore down his bronze statue and dug up his buried leg, dragging it through the streets on a rope. Gen. José Joaquín Herrera was named interim president in December 1844.

In January 1845, Santa Anna fled to Mexico's gulf coast, where a group of Indians captured him, recognizing him by his wooden leg. Santa Anna found himself imprisoned at Fort Perote nearby. From there, he was allowed to go into exile in Havana, Cuba.

Santa Anna's offer to acknowledge the independence of Texas did not reach Washington officials until January 1845. A month later, outgoing President Tyler pushed the joint resolution for Texas's annexation through Congress. Further action was stalled when legislators realized the Constitution had no such provision for this method of getting territory. How should they formally bring Texas into the Union? The answer to that question was left to Tyler's successor, James Polk, who had assumed office in March 1845.

Polk, also influenced by Andrew Jackson, passionately favored annexation. But he was more interested in another Mexican state, California. Texas included, after all, large expanses of sparsely populated

John Slidell, a lawyer in New Orleans, was sent to Mexico in December 1845 with the authority to offer $40 million to purchase the Mexican-held lands north of the Rio Grande, but he had no success and returned in March 1846. *(Library of Congress)*

desert. Moreover, rumor leaked out that General Herrera, the Mexican president, might be willing to sell California. With that news, Polk met with his cabinet on September 16, 1845. They unanimously voted to send John Slidell of New Orleans down to Mexico City to offer up to $40 million for upper California and as much of the Southwest as they could get.

On the one hand, Mexico was asked to receive special commissioner Slidell to resolve differences over Texas (and slyly try to buy California); on the other, Gen. Zachary Taylor was ordered to go "as near to the Rio Grande as circumstances permit" and prepare for battle. As if that were not enough, U.S. Navy captain Robert Stockton, an extreme expansionist, was sent at the head of a fleet to loiter off the Pacific Coast. Then he would be ordered to back up a local uprising, land his marines, and thus win a war in California. Polk was covering all possibilities.

Mexico's President Herrera faced a dilemma. If he refused the offer to sell California, the North Americans might start a war. On the other hand, if he tried to sell California and that news got out, another revolution might start in Mexico. Indeed, on the very day President Polk signed the act admitting Texas to the Union—December 29, 1845—and just as Slidell was to arrive in Mexico City, Herrera was overthrown by General Paredes himself. Paredes was all for war against the United States and refused to accept Slidell as a legitimate U.S. agent. "Be assured," wrote Slidell arrogantly, "that nothing is to be done with these people, until they have been chastised [punished]." Meanwhile, the Mexican press trumpeted: "We have more than enough strength to make war. Let us make it then, and victory will perch upon our banners!" Slidell waited in Mexico City for further orders. He tried on March 1, 1846, to gain an audience with Paredes, was refused March 12, and left for home on March 21.

In exile on Cuba, the sly Santa Anna tried another approach. Through a Mexican friend, Col. Alexander J. Atocha, he sent a message to Washington in February 1846. Santa Anna said that he approved of Paredes's revolution and knew that Paredes would agree to the Rio Grande boundary and to giving up some of California for the price of $30 million. Polk, Santa Anna suggested, must apply force and give Paredes a reason to give in. Why did Santa Anna say such things—in effect, probably outright lies? It seems he wanted to knock out the opposition (Paredes) who, by now, wanted a Mexican monarchy. Then Santa Anna hoped to march into Mexico, once more, as a conquering hero.

All this, then—and more—had gone on behind the scenes before Taylor and Mexican general Pedro de Ampudia faced off at Matamoros and the call to arms was made official. On May 10, 1846, President Polk's war message was read to an agitated legislature. News of the hostilities at Matamoros had reached Congress, and the noise of debate in the hall was thunderous, fired by deep disagreements. The Democrats—Polk's party—supported the war and the Whigs—Polk's opposition—were divided.

All that was needed was Congress's vote to make the war official, but it took two days of bitter debate. "Landjobbers! Slavejobbers!" shouted the antiwar faction. Their basic position was that Polk and his cronies only wanted more and more land that they could fill with more and more slaves. Opponents leapt to their feet, shouting in rebuttal.

As always with politicians, there were sleight-of-hand deals and heavy-handed persuasions. One of the leaders of the opposition to a war was the aging former president, still a representative from

Massachusetts, John Quincy Adams. Finally Adams switched, fearing crippling divisions of the Union. This infuriated his antiwar constituents. That July 4, Charles Sumner of Massachusetts exclaimed, "Blood! Blood! is on the hands of representatives from Boston," as he railed against the lack of firm conviction among his colleagues (such as Adams) who allowed the war to go on.

Although it took two days, on May 12, 1846, the angry, bitterly divided 29th Congress finally gave the war bill their "yeas"—174 against the 14 nays in the House, 40-2 in the Senate. These "thumping majorities," as daily newspapers dubbed these votes, immediately proceeded to vote enthusiastically for a draft of 50,000 men and authorized $10 million to start the war effort. Polk and his supporters now had their war with Mexico.

WAR ALONG THE
RIO GRANDE

In the 1840s, messages traveled slowly, but in April 1846 Gen. Zachary Taylor was in no mood to wait for word from Washington to wage a campaign. Eager to continue direct action against the Mexicans, he would join in three battles with the Mexicans along the Rio Grande even before word of war was official. Some members of Congress and their constituents suspected that Polk himself was quite happy to have Taylor go ahead with the war, declared or not, with or without approval from Washington.

Before Polk signed the War Bill on May 13, and before official notice of the signing reached Taylor at the end of May, Mexican and U.S. troops played a slow-motion cat-and-mouse game. U.S. troops at the border by this time numbered only some 3,900, while there were about 5,700 Mexican troops in the immediate vicinity.

On April 26, Taylor notified Washington of the events near Matamoros. On April 30, General Arista ordered a caravan of about 1,600 soldiers and as many arms and supplies as his wagons could carry to cross the Rio Grande at Longoreno, below Matamoros. The overfilled carts lurched through the shallows of the broad river, then lurched back again for another load. Arista lacked enough transport equipment to move more soldiers or more arms at one time.

General Taylor got news of Arista's movements. At Fort Texas, across the river from the Mexican town of Matamoros, Taylor left the weak and sick behind with only a few soldiers to guard them. Then he made a forced 18-mile march with 3,000 troops toward Point Isabel at the mouth of the Rio Grande.

Arista doubled back behind his enemy and, on May 3, surrounded Fort Texas. When the Mexican sent a message to the U.S. garrison, asking the fort's commander, Capt. Edgar Hawkins, not to resist, he

Western Territories and Spanish Possessions, 1820–1845

BRITISH TERRITORY

Oregon Country
Joint U.S.-British occupation

Missouri R.

Unorganized Territory

Iowa Territory 1838

Wisconsin Territory 1836

Lake Superior

Michigan Territory 1836

Lake Huron

(Michigan 1837)

Lake Michigan

Great Salt Lake

Colorado R.

1837

Illinois

Indiana

MEXICO
Independent from Spain 1821

Claimed by Mexico and Texas

Missouri 1821

Kentucky

PACIFIC OCEAN

Arkansas R.

Arkansas Territory 1819

Arkansas 1836

Tennessee

Red R.

Alabama

Missis-sippi

N

Rio Grande

REPUBLIC OF TEXAS 1836

(TEXAS 1845)

Louisiana

Gulf of Mexico

| 0 | 300 miles |
| 0 | 300 km |

| | U.S. territory | | British territory | | Joint occupation | | Spanish territory | | Disputed territory |

1821 Date of statehood or territorial organization

© Infobase Publishing

replied: "The exact purport of your despatch I cannot feel confident that I understand, as my interpreter is not skilled in your language, but if I have understood you correctly, my reply is that I must respectfully decline to surrender." With that, he and his men started tearing up tents for sandbags and got ready to sit out the siege. Among the first few who lost their lives as the siege began was Maj. Jacob Brown. The U.S. troops renamed the fort after him; later, it became the site of present-day Brownsville, Texas.

On May 6, recruits from New Orleans arrived at Point Isabel, whose harbor opened onto the Gulf of Mexico. Five hundred navy and marine troops, under Commodore David Conner, disembarked. Perhaps encouraged by knowledge that 500 more troops were there if he needed them, Taylor then led a cumbersome train of 300 wagons and 3,500 troops out of Point Isabel west toward Matamoros and Fort Brown.

On May 8, Taylor spied Arista and his troops through the wavering heat of midday. The Mexicans had positioned themselves at the edge of a woods, on the plains of Palo Alto, north of Matamoros on the Texas side. All along the enemy line, General Arista trotted back and forth in front of his troops. American observers claimed that they heard him shout slogans like *"Viva la Revolución! Viva México!"* to cheer them on. Then, when the two armies were only half a mile apart, Mexico's big guns snarled and blasted cannon shot in the direction of the U.S. troops. The Mexicans' powder was damp and the artillery more cumberstone than efficient. A rapid American cannonade strafed the Mexican front line. Hardly any infantry was engaged, and neither side so much as touched each other with bayonets, knives, or bare hands. But one thing was quite clear. From the beginning, the North American troops had superior firepower.

One hour later, the prairie grass burst into flame and smoke completely blanketed the area between the armies. Although there were

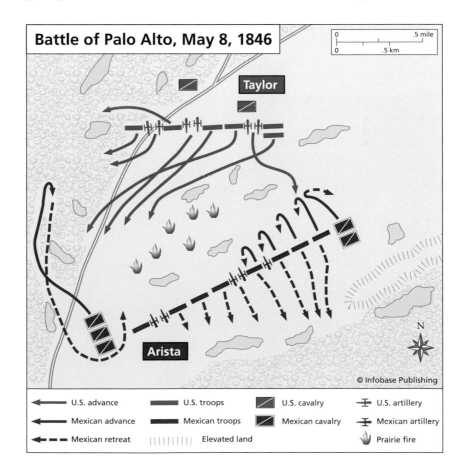

Battle of Palo Alto, May 8, 1846

0   .5 mile
0   .5 km

Taylor

Arista

N

© Infobase Publishing

⟵ U.S. advance	▬ U.S. troops	▨ U.S. cavalry	⊥ U.S. artillery
⟵ Mexican advance	▬ Mexican troops	▨ Mexican cavalry	⊥ Mexican artillery
⟵ - - Mexican retreat	‖‖‖‖‖‖ Elevated land		♨ Prairie fire

some troop movement and some firing after the blaze died down, night ended the fray. No one was sure who had won. One U.S. soldier fled in terror from camp that night, and he ran all the way to Commodore Conner's navy troops at Point Isabel to say that the battle was wild and bloody. This so excited the forces at Point Isabel that they wanted to leave that instant to help Taylor's men. Conner restrained them.

In fact, at Palo Alto that May 8, only 44 U.S. troops were wounded and nine killed, compared to the 250 Mexican casualties. It was the custom in those days to treat all wounded, friend or foe, and the procession of sufferers carried off the field on stretchers was lengthy. Taylor recalled in his letters, "The surgeon's saw was going the livelong night."

At the next battle, on May 9, U.S. regulars easily won in Resaca de Palma, an area just south of Palo Alto, but still on the Texas side of the river. *Resacas* are old stream beds, and the surrounding terrain is irregular and perfect for hand-to-hand combat. At almost every turn, Taylor positioned his army so that it was protected. Then he directed his

On May 8, 1846, at Palo Alto, U.S. and Mexican forces fought the first major battle of the war. *(Library of Congress)*

The fall of Major Samuel Ringgold at the Battle of Palo Alto *(National Archives)*

artillery to back up his infantrymen. Though gun-shy after the massive cannon attack of the previous day, the Mexicans fought bravely. As they captured some U.S. artillery, it was reported that Taylor shouted at his Eighth Infantry and part of the Fifth, "Take those guns, and by God keep them!" They did.

Throughout the battle, Taylor sat on his horse, Old Whitey, with one leg hooked around the pommel of his saddle, as he directed the action. Behind the Mexican lines, General Arista sat in his tent doing paperwork. He was unaware that this battle was anything more than a "skirmish," until his troops broke and he was forced to flee without his writing desk and other baggage. Two hundred sixty-two Mexicans were killed, 355 wounded, 185 were missing, and many more drowned in the swift currents of the Rio Grande, as they struggled to escape by crossing the river. Stragglers were picked off as they passed by Fort Texas, which had successfully survived the siege. U.S. casualties at Resaca de Palma were 33 killed and 89 wounded.

Rather than pursue them, Taylor set up camp on the spot. On the night of May 9, as Polk was finishing up his message to Congress to plead for a declaration of war, Taylor wrote in his journal, "Camp 3 miles from Matamoros, 10 P.M. The enemy has recrossed the river and I am sure will not again molest us on this bank." He was right, and in the following battles, it was the American general who pursued the Mexicans—and far below the Rio Grande.

While Taylor was planning his next move against the Mexicans, on May 13, 1846, Polk signed the War Bill that marked the official beginning of the U.S.-Mexican War, or, to the Mexicans, *La Guerra de Defensa* ("the war of defense"). Upon signing, Polk remarked that he wanted, "a small war, just large enough to require a treaty of peace, and not large enough to make military reputations." Although some have interpreted that remark as evidence that Polk sincerely wanted to avoid a major conflict with Mexico, others see it as suggesting that Polk did not want any war heroes to run against him in the next election.

Whatever his motives, Polk did hesitate to make the choice of commander of the U.S. Army about to wage war against Mexico. Polk distrusted Taylor's leadership abilities—Taylor was not a West Point graduate but had advanced through the ranks by virtue of his battlefield experience. Not for nothing was he known as "Old Rough and Ready." The other obvious candidate was Gen. Winfield Scott, general in chief of the army and a veteran of the War of 1812 and the Indian wars. But Scott, aside from his reputation of being egotistical and outspoken, was suspected of being politically ambitious. Indeed, Scott wanted to be a hero and he clearly envied Taylor's victories. This created a strain between the two military men, as Scott agitated to be sent to Mexico.

In the end, Polk avoided a confrontation. He promoted the less heroic-appearing man, Gen. Zachary Taylor, to major general for his "gallant victories" and appointed him to command the Army of the Rio Grande. Scott was verbally promised that he would eventually command the main assault on Mexico but meanwhile he was assigned temporarily to train enlistees in Virginia. For "Old Fuss and Feathers," as Scott was sometimes called, Polk's decision was not a happy one.

While the difficulties of assigning military command temporarily settled, Polk turned his attention to strategy. The goal for Polk and his cabinet was to create a threefold force: an "Army of the West," to conquer New Mexico and California; an "Army of the Center," to keep Chihuahua and northern Mexico under control; and an "Army of Occupation," to march for Mexico City and determine the terms of peace. Gen. Stephen Kearny was assigned to oversee the western front (California), General John Wool would head up the Army of the Center, and Taylor was to head up the army that would presumably be

assigned eventually to march on Mexico City—the exact route, timing, and tactics were still vague.

Taylor had more immediate concerns. On May 17 and 18, 1846, Taylor's opponent, General Arista, evacuated the Mexican town of Matamoros. Then Arista's troops seemed to disappear into the desert, as Taylor crossed the Rio Grande on May 18. According to the diary entry of one recruit, the invading U.S. army found "nothing but old hags, worse-looking than Indians." But having taken official possession of the town and with news of his recent conquests making headlines, the 61-year-old Taylor, despite his stubby body and unkempt clothes, became an overnight hero in the United States. Tailors scrambled to fill orders for clothes like Taylor's ragged pantaloons and ratty brown jacket for fashion-conscious admirers.

Arista's troops, however, did not just evaporate into the desert. Rather, they struggled through it. They killed raft animals for food and—being short on water—for animals' precious blood. Soldiers carried their own saddles and gear. On May 28, 1846, they finally arrived in the Mexican town of Linares. From Linares, nearly 100 miles southwest of Matamoros, it was an easy march to either Victoria, the inland capital city of the Mexican state, Tamaulipas, or to Monterrey, capital of Nuevo Leon.

So it seemed that Taylor's front was locating itself in present-day northeastern Mexico, in the state of Tamaulipas—and as U.S. strategy would dictate. But his departure from Matamoros was agonizingly slow. In Matamoros, indignities against civilians continued; during Taylor's occupation of the town, even more disgusted U.S. recruits defected to the renegade San Patricio Brigade.

Meanwhile, more and more U.S. volunteers poured into Taylor's garrisons at Matamoros. Indeed, troops came from all over the country, but most came from the South and what is now the Midwest. On May 22, Louisiana troops arrived by boat. At the same time, "Gaines's Army" (named after the general who recruited them) arrived from the Mississippi Valley for a six months' tour of duty. Taylor had not even asked for them. Untrained, unwilling to stay longer, most were soon sent home, and the expression, "just like Gaines's Army" came to mean a useless attempt.

As June wore on, Taylor spent his time not in readying the new recruits for battle or in the glorious pursuit of victory, but in the dull and frustrating task of seeking out transport equipment. In particular, boats were in short supply, and Taylor needed these to carry volunteers and equipment from New Orleans to the mouth of the Rio Grande and then up the shallow river to Matamoros. Army suppliers were also short of mules, the preferred beasts of burden in this war.

Even before Taylor crossed the Rio Grande, hospital supplies and tents for the ordinary soldier grew scarce. And what goods did appear were often of poor quality. Indeed:

> Two-thirds of the tents furnished the army . . . were worn out and rotten . . . [and so] For days and weeks every article in hundreds of tents was thoroughly soaked. During those terrible months, the suffering of the sick in the crowded hospital tents were horrible beyond conception.

wrote one young artillery officer around the time when troops were deployed at Corpus Christi, still on the Texas side of the Rio Grande. After three battles, the process of equipping the army for combat and its accompanying tasks still dragged, and Taylor became more and more frustrated with the snail's pace of it all.

Clearly the U.S. Army was poorly prepared for the war it now found itself engaged in. (The navy and marines were not much better prepared at the outset, but they would play only supporting roles and they had time to get themselves better equipped.) Except for the relatively minor conflicts with Indians—the Seminole of Florida and the so-called Black Hawk War—the U.S. Army had not been called on to fight a war since the last shot in the War of 1812 was fired at New Orleans in January 1815. Americans as a people had hoped to escape the wars that so divided Europe, and most had little interest in maintaining a large professional army. In the interests of economy, the regular army had been drastically cut back in size, especially since 1842.

This reluctance to spend money on an army was reflected in the inconsistency of the arms and weapons carried by the troops at the outset of the war. Most soldiers carried their own knives—the long, sharp, steel-bladed bowie knife or some variation—which were used to perform all kinds of practical tasks more often than in hand-to-hand fighting. Bayonets attached to the barrel of muskets or rifles were the preferred weapon in the latter situation. Officers still carried swords, mostly for ceremony but also occasionally to be used in close combat. The cavalry had sabers, heavy-duty curved swords with hand guards that protected them if they had to slash their way through enemy troops.

Many soldiers, those of lower rank as well as officers, also carried pistols, usually old-fashioned single-shot pistols with either flintlock or percussion caps to ignite the charge. But in the later stages of the war, a few lucky men—mostly cavalry and officers—would be issued the new Colt revolver. Although there had been several types of revolving firearms over the centuries, Samuel Colt, a young Connecticut inventor,

SAMUEL COLT AND HIS SIX-SHOOTER

Fascinated by explosives, Samuel Colt (1814–62) acquired his first pistol at age seven; at 10, while living in Ware, Massachusetts, he launched a spectacular explosion in Ware Pond. Later, enrolled at nearby Amherst Academy, his July 4, 1830, attempt at a fireworks display ignited a school building. His father hastily packed him off on a boat to Calcutta as a common seaman. There Colt carved a wooden model of his first revolving, multibarrel, single-action pistol, designed to fire five shots in 20 seconds.

Raising money by promoting nitrous oxide (laughing gas), Colt patented his revolver in 1835 and opened a firearms company in Paterson, New Jersey. His weapons saw some service in the Second Seminole Indian War and the Texas rebellion against Mexico, but business failed in 1842. By 1845, however, the Texas Rangers were favoring the Colt revolver, by then six-barreled. In 1846, Colt scrambled to fill the U.S. military's sudden order for 1,000 of these "six-shooters." Colt's revolver cannot claim to have won the war, but the war made its reputation.

This print shows Samuel Colt holding an early model of the revolver he invented and that was a prized weapon in the war against Mexico. *(Library of Congress)*

had patented the first truly practical revolving firearm in 1835; Colt's invention was to rotate the cartridge cylinder with each cock of the hammer. Colt's revolver was slow to gain acceptance—the U.S. Army in those days was very conservative when it came to adopting new weapons—and Colt's first factory failed in 1842. With the outbreak of the war in Mexico, however, and because of some improvements in the Colt revolver, the U.S. Army ordered 1,000 of these "six-shooters" in 1846 and these soon won favor among the troops. Other orders quickly followed, and the Colt revolver emerged from the Mexican War as the pistol of choice for many Americans.

The standard weapon issued to the infantry was a musket—smoothbore, single-shot, muzzle-loaded, using either flintlock or percussion caps. The main limitation of such a musket was that it was not very accurate or effective over 100 yards. The army also issued some rifles—the muzzle-loading type made at the Harpers Ferry armory, the breech-loading flintlock Hall's rifle, or the percussion-cap Model 1841 (also known as the "Mississippi Rifle" or the "Yager"). The Remington-Jenks bolt-action, breech-loading rifle also was used by some in the Mexican War and, of course, many volunteers and militia carried their own favorite locally made muskets and rifles. Rifles, with the spiral grooves in their barrels, were more effective over longer distances but were slower in operation than muskets.

The artillery relied mainly on two types of pieces—cannons or howitzers. The latter are relatively small, stubby cannons that are pointed at angles so that their projectiles arc at higher elevations and thus go over obstacles such as ridges to reach the enemy's position. (A "mountain howitzer" was simply a lighter type that could be more easily carried over difficult terrain.) The cannons, most of which were muzzle-loaded, fired in a relatively straight line and were rated by the weight of the projectile they fired—from four-pounders all the way up to 24-pounders. On special occasions such as besieging forts or cities, the army would call on the navy and use its heavy 32-pounders or even 68-pounders. Most of the shot were simply large iron balls, but there were also such varieties as chain shot (two shells linked by a short chain that ripped through anything in its way), canister (iron balls in a light cylindrical casing that bursts on the firing) and grapeshot (usually nine small iron balls held together by iron plates and exploding on contact).

Just supplying all the types of ammunition needed by all these different weapons put a tremendous strain on the resources and logistical capabilities of the U.S. government. One of the factors that worked in favor of the U.S. Army in the early months of the war was that the Mexicans had their own share of troubles. As Taylor and his armies threatened the northern part of the country, weak leadership in the Mexican government kept the whole nation in turmoil. When news of Palo Alto, Resaca de Palma, and the retreat of the Mexican army reached the capital, it angered Mexican citizens so much that they began to rebel against their president, Mariano Paredes y Arrillaga and his Conservative Party.

Of course, this internal struggle did not go unnoticed in the United States. Even as the U.S. Congress debated Polk's War Bill in May, the president planned a secret approach to none other than the wily chameleon, Gen. Antonio López de Santa Anna. For, as legislators wrangled, Polk gave secret orders to the navy: If Santa Anna should try to come back home from Havana, let the exiled despot through. Polk remembered Santa Anna's desperate attempts to stay in power, even at the cost of giving away part of Mexico; and the U.S. president thought time might be ripe for a U.S.-controlled leader in Mexico City.

President James K. Polk (1795–1849) during the 1840s *(National Archives)*

But Mexican unrest was so severe that even the swaggering Santa Anna hesitated. Cautiously, he tried to assess the safest moment for a triumphant return. Finally, in June 1846, as General Taylor at last saw the possibility of moving into Mexico with adequate military supplies, Polk sent a mission to Havana with Alexander Slidell MacKenzie, the young navy commander and nephew of John Slidell, acting as U.S. representative. Over tea and cakes—and perhaps a little rum—MacKenzie tried to make a deal: Santa Anna of course remembered the offer he made to the United States this past February, to support the recognition of the Rio Grande as the border of Texas and surrender of part of California to the United States? President Polk was now prepared to accept this offer, and if Santa Anna was agreeable to it, Polk would also be happy to support the general's return to power and to pay "generously." Santa Anna smiled in agreement and suggested that U.S. troops take a few more cities and defeat Paredes, for the Mexican president was still fighting to hang on to his office. Then, Santa Anna predicted, Mexico would complete its revolt and recall the old war hero—himself—back to power.

On July 1, 1846, the Mexican congress formally declared war. With Matamoros secure, Taylor and his army began pushing southward along the San Juan valley toward Camargo, a small town some 75 miles west along the river. But troop discipline under Taylor remained a problem. According to one officer's diary,

> We reached Burrita about 5 p.m., many of the Louisiana volunteers were there, a lawless drunken rabble. They had driven away the inhabitants, taken possession of their houses, and were emulating each other in making beasts of themselves.

Looking back at the U.S.-Mexican War from the perspective of 1892, the same John L. O'Sullivan who thundered proudly about Manifest Destiny would comment,

> The regulars regarded the volunteers with impatience and contempt . . . [The volunteers] robbed Mexicans of their cattle and corn, stole their fences for firewood, got drunk, and killed several inoffensive inhabitants of the town in the streets.

Officers' memoirs describe behavior much worse than that—scalping innocent civilians, killing women, children, and babies, burning

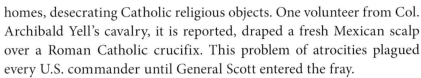

homes, desecrating Catholic religious objects. One volunteer from Col. Archibald Yell's cavalry, it is reported, draped a fresh Mexican scalp over a Roman Catholic crucifix. This problem of atrocities plagued every U.S. commander until General Scott entered the fray.

The climate, too, had its revenge. Although some of the U.S. troops moved up the Rio Grande and occupied the riverside town of Camargo on July 14, it was more than a month before Taylor moved the rest of his troops and all of his supplies to the town. By then, the heat soared, the water went foul, and the soldiers contracted diarrhea, dysentery, and all sorts of diseases from bad hygiene and unsafe drinking water. Some regiments lost a third of their men.

Still Santa Anna did not leave Havana. Suspecting Santa Anna's sincerity, Polk sent a peace proposal to Paredes by way of Commodore Conner on July 27. But it would not arrive in Mexico City until August 30, and by that time, much would have happened. For one, Commodore Conner took time out from his duties as a messenger to open a naval attack on the port town of Alvarado, located about 30 miles from Veracruz. On August 6, Conner failed to navigate past the strong currents at the mouth of the Alvarado River. With bad weather threatening, the expedition foundered.

Another intervening event was a legislative conflict that began on August 8 when one of Polk's Democrats introduced the "Two Million Bill" to the House. Not counting on the peace overtures made to Paredes, either, Polk tried raising money for his war and for Santa Anna's payoff for his collaboration with the United States. But when President Polk asked Congress for $2 million, his requests were ripped to shreds as the prowar and the antiwar factions in Congress battled each other. Even the Whig party of Massachusetts was split into two camps, "Cotton" and "Conscience," based on whether or not members sided with the prowar slave interests ("Cotton").

The hot Washington August just made matters more intense, and it was the end of that year's session. From August 4 to 10, the atmosphere in Congress was wild; everyone wanted to go home. Then David Wilmot, representative from Pennsylvania, proposed an amendment banning slavery from any Mexican territory the United States might win. The overwhelming majority of antislavery representatives, both Whigs and Northern Democrats, shouted a "Yea!" vote. Proslavery representatives thundered opposition. Other supporters of the Two Million Bill—without the Wilmot Proviso, as the amendment was called—popped up.

On August 10, 1846, Congress finally adjourned, without pass-
ing the bill. But it would not be the last of the Wilmot Proviso. Polk's
secretary of the treasury, Robert J. Walker of Mississippi, sank into a
terrible mood. The president's "small war" was dragging. It was unjust,
complained the secretary, that the Mexicans kept fighting so persis-
tently. The financial burden they imposed on the United States would
"compel us to overthrow our own financial policy and arrest this great
nation in her high and prosperous career," Walker grumbled.

General Taylor, on the other hand, was still trying to wage a war.
As the general moved southwest, Monterrey, capital of Nuevo Leon,
loomed on the horizon. Farther south lay Tamaulipas and its capital,
Victoria. Mexico's Arista and his forces were at Linares to the north,
within easy reach of both Monterrey and Victoria. What would be
the best course of action? Taylor decided that Monterrey would be his
next target and, on August 10, as the Two Million Bill foundered in
Congress, Taylor sent one of his Texas Rangers ahead to reconnoiter
the area.

Taylor's plan was to proceed southwest toward Monterrey through
the tiny towns of Mier and Cerralvo. On August 17, 1846, one division
under Brig. Gen. William Worth took the lead toward Cerralvo, and
several units followed. The total number of men marching was 6,000—
half volunteer and half regular.

So many of the troops that followed from Camargo to Monterrey
were still ill and dying, according to one officer, that the road was "slip-
pery with . . . foam and blood." One group marching from Camargo
grimly renamed themselves the First Diarrhea Rangers. Yet, even with
a weakened army and the problem of transporting the materials of war,
no one opposed their march toward the spot where they hoped to begin
a major attack.

At the same time, toward the end of that August 1846, the conservative Paredes finally fell. No one in the new Mexican government was
interested in the U.S. peace proposals. Rather, they all wanted to battle
the United States. Santa Anna, the hero of the revolution and their
best general, was asked to come home—just as the general himself had
predicted.

Thus, pretending to return to Mexico City so he could make peace
for the *norteamericanos,* Santa Anna slipped through the naval blockade of Veracruz on August 16. Once through, he began acting quite
differently than the United States might have expected. He blustered

MILITARY MEDICINE DURING TAYLOR'S CAMPAIGN

Disease laid the U.S. troops low, even before they suffered from war wounds. Measles, mumps, diarrhea, and fever, combined with badly trained doctors and support staff, negligible hygiene, bad water, no immunizations—all caused seven times more losses than did combat. All of these could be—and often were—fatal; malaria and yellow fever especially were notorious killers.

Medical treatment was not specific to the condition and was geared only to symptom relief. Bloodletting was a prevailing treatment in those days for all manner of ailments and was even used after amputation, when physicians thought it best to remove about the same amount of blood as circulated in the missing limb. In the case of dysentery and diarrhea, one prominent physician recommended bleeding every two or three days.

More so than did civilian doctors, army physicians used other methods. Their pharmacopoeia included quinine sulfate for malaria. Supplies did not always get through, though, so sulfate of zinc or myrrh, sometimes with opium, was substituted. One doctor, when sulfate of zinc ran out, substituted arsenic. Other doctors treated dysentery/diarrhea with gentle emetics of dry roasted rhubarb, ipecacuanha (an herb), and opium. Calomel, or mercury chloride, was also popular. And in the absence of all these, created glass of antimony—possibly a soluble form of the ore—was used to treat dysentery.

For yellow fever, mustard plasters and a warm mustard bath were part of treatment. Indeed, yellow fever was especially feared. One of four patients died of it, and no one connected it with the mosquito, although General Scott had his army clear rotting vegetables and animal carcasses off the streets of Veracruz, unwittingly reducing insect breeding areas.

Medical reports, the few that were completed, were inept. Homesick recruits were not above faking illness. Still the mortality rate was verifiably high; only luck prevailed. "Even the birds learned to sing the funeral march," wrote one recruit, claiming that mockingbirds actually learned to sing the funeral dirge as part of their repertoire.

into the capital, bragging that he had a force of 25,000 men, all ready to pursue the hated Taylor. (In fact, it took him until January 1847 to raise an army of 18,000.) To those who heard him, he did not sound like he was going to be a tool of the U.S. government.

On August 30, as the U.S. peace offer to Paredes finally reached the capital, Santa Anna joined the newly elected cabinet as head of the Mexican armed forces. José Mariano Salas became acting president, Valentín Gómez Farías, vice president.

Still, the Mexican people were not so enthusiastic about Santa Anna's return as the old war hero might have believed. They remembered his love for power very well. Santa Anna was arrogant and corrupt. He loved fancy possessions, young girls, opium, and, above all, glory. Modeling his army after the army of the French hero Napoléon, he immodestly called himself "the Napoléon of the West." Unfortunately, he was all the Mexicans had at that time.

Now, actively recruiting an opposing Mexican force to fight the United States, Santa Anna neither informed Washington of his activities nor immediately charged out of the capital with a bristling army of 25,000. And no one in Washington knew that the Mexican general had tricked them.

Despite several other behind-the-scenes efforts to disrupt Mexico in a nonmilitary way, the U.S. cabinet pored over its maps, planning campaign after campaign. Taylor, in the meantime, was waging his own campaign almost completely ignorant of what Washington was doing. At this time his campaign consisted of marching his army toward Monterrey.

General Taylor arrives at Monterrey, September 19, 1846. *(Library of Congress)*

In September 1846, Gen. Zachary Taylor commanded the siege and capture of Monterrey, a major city in northeastern Mexico. *(Library of Congress)*

Thus, on September 19, 1846, Taylor and his advancing army camped with the stone buildings of Monterrey in full view. Neither aware that Polk had made several diplomatic maneuvers to force Mexico's hand, nor aware that Santa Anna had returned, Taylor and his army readied for battle. The Mexican force at Monterrey was led by Taylor's old foe, General Ampudia.

Taylor now divided his forces in two, putting himself in charge of one and General Worth in charge of the other. The tension in both Mexican and U.S. camps grew. Facing the gates of the city, members of Taylor's Texas cavalry flung themselves up on their horses and thundered straight toward the opposition, just to get a look at the Mexicans. At the last moment, they wheeled around and galloped back to safety in a cloud of dust and laughter. It must have driven the Mexican forces mad with anticipation.

On the eve of the battle, as Taylor sat poised at the gates of Monterrey, the news of Santa Anna's betrayal reached Washington. President Polk was livid. But more than his distress at Santa Anna, he worried about his chief commander of the force in Mexico, General Taylor. With little thought regarding the difficulties of communications at such long distances, and in the wee hours of the night, he had confided to his diary:

General Taylor . . . gives but little information. He seems to act like a regular soldier, whose only duty is to obey orders and seems . . . to avoid all responsibility of making any suggestions or giving any opinions.

Meanwhile, in the dim light of an early Mexican morning, on September 20, 1846, Gen. Zachary Taylor sent Worth circling westward to attack Monterrey from that direction while Taylor was to attack head on from the east. An estimated 5,000 to 7,000 Mexican troops held them off for a day, but under withering attack by Worth, the western part of the city gave way the next day. Retreating to the heart of Monterrey, the Mexicans found themselves surrounded. Finally, on September 24, the white flag of surrender went up in the *zócalo,* the center of the city.

General Taylor and his U.S. forces could now boast that they had captured the provincial Mexican city of Monterrey—but at a waste of lives on all sides. Some 800 U.S. soldiers were killed or wounded (no precise accounting was ever provided), while the Mexicans lost probably twice as many. It was also a waste of time—five months. It appeared that the road to Mexico City was going to be long and arduous and that President Polk's "small war" was going to be very costly indeed.

The last day of the siege of Monterrey, September 24, 1846 *(National Archives)*

The U.S. flag is displayed prominently in this lithograph of Monterrey. *(Library of Congress)*

And while Taylor's army and its supporting forces were so engaged in that remote corner of Mexico, Americans were also involved in fighting Mexicans to gain control of another part of the former Nueva España—California and the Southwest.

CALIFORNIA AND THE SOUTHWEST

Almost simultaneous with Taylor's early battles in northeast Mexico, yet in some ways almost independent of that war with Mexico, the United States would forcibly take over the vast Mexican provinces of California and New Mexico. This seizure involved some complicated events and featured some remarkable characters. And while the war in Mexico often seemed remote, a series of battles fought by isolated soldiers, the war in California and the Southwest seemed to mesh with larger patterns of U.S. history.

California, for example, had long appealed to U.S. citizens, quite aside from any current desire to take territory from Mexico and give it to the United States. In the 1840s, as in decades to come, North Americans saw it as the land of milk and honey, a fertile, beautiful place for easy living.

In the early 1840s, a handsome adventurer and officer in the U.S. Army's Corps of Topographical Engineers, John C. Frémont, enlarged that myth. His wife, Jessie Frémont, collaborated on a best-selling account of her husband's 1842 exploration of the Pacific Northwest that whetted expansionists' appetites, including the appetite of Frémont's father-in-law, Missouri senator Thomas Hart Benton, who helped Frémont organize another expedition in 1843. On this adventure, caught in bad weather in the Sierras, Frémont headed south into California, which was then a Mexican state.

For several months in 1844, Frémont explored northern California all the way to the San Francisco Bay area, and on his return to Washington, he and Jessie collaborated on another exciting account. Since he portrayed a land where Mexico had little control or even presence, many U.S. legislators who favored the Mexican War and U.S. possession of California grew wild with anticipation.

John C. Frémont (1813–90) was on a U.S. Army mapping expedition in the West when the war with Mexico broke out. Resigning his commission, he became a leader of the California Anglos, who rose up against Mexico. *(Library of Congress)*

President Polk wanted the California that lay between San Diego and the Oregon boundary, and he wanted the Mexican province of New Mexico—the latter roughly covering New Mexico, Nevada, Arizona, Utah, and parts of Colorado and Wyoming of today. In fact, on March 30, 1846, even before the war with Mexico officially began, the president confided to his diary that he wanted not only California, he wanted Texas and everything in between, "due west to the Pacific."

Polk's desire was not original; it was an enormously popular idea. Typically, one starry-eyed young naval officer traveling with the Pacific Squadron to Monterey, California, put it even more enthusiastically:

> Asia will be brought to our very doors. Population will flow into the fertile regions of California. The resources of the entire country will be developed. The public lands lying along the railways will be changed from deserts into gardens, and a large population will be settled.

Thus, a new kind of settler started to fill the part of California above Sacramento to the Oregon border ("Alto," or Northern, California). Believing in Manifest Destiny, these U.S. settlers had no interest in mixing with the Californians—the Mexicans, Anglo-Mexicans, or Native Americans—already there. Rather than build communities, they came to get rich from land, fur trading, whatever was quick.

Frémont, whatever his flaws, was motivated by other desires. Full of high spirits and the lust for fame, Frémont set out in June 1845 on what was publicly announced as an official mapmaking expedition. But he also received secret orders from Washington to keep an eye on the British—Polk worried that they might intervene on behalf of Mexico—and to encourage Californians to accept a U.S. takeover. When he arrived at the Oregon-California border in April of 1846, U.S. naval forces, under Commodore John Sloat, were off Mexico's western coast, and Frémont's appearance seemed hardly coincidental.

On May 13, 1846, the United States officially declared war against Mexico, and the newspapers soon filled with accounts of General Taylor's glorious victories. On the verge of an agreement with the United States about Oregon, Britain had no desire to go to battle with the United States over California or any other Mexican territory.

Among those in California, rumors of war had been circulating for some time in the settlers' camps along the California-Oregon border long before Frémont arrived in April. But a counter rumor also spread that local (Mexican) officials planned to get rid of the new arrivals by stirring up Native Americans to attack them.

Frémont had shown up ready for adventure and, convinced that he had the support of President Polk, he resigned his commission in the U.S. Army so as to appear to be leading a civilian uprising. Taking his bravado as a sign that the U.S. government was behind him, the new Anglo settlers immediately joined him in attacking the territory's Mexican governors.

On June 10, 1846, the rebels seized a herd of horses meant for one of the local officials. Then they took the town of Sonoma, captured a town official, General Mariano Vallejo, and several other residents. Vallejo had been sympathetic to the Anglo-Americans, but after Frémont and his men took him and his brother to Sutter's Fort—the main outpost of the Anglo community in northern California—and roughed them up, the Vallejos were sympathetic no more.

The Anglos rode behind a crude flag that showed an awkward shape of a bear—maybe a brown grizzly, a stripe made from a bright bit of ribbon, and the Lone Star of Texas. It was not the first time Mexicans had seen it, for in 1832, Anglo-Texas had raised such a flag with a bear on it, protesting the excise taxes of their host country. This time, it was Frémont who, completely without authorization, rode with the bear flag fluttering at the head of a motley crew of opportunists in what historians later dubbed "The Bear Flag Rebellion." Together he and the rebels took over an empty fort in the Mexican settlement of San Francisco.

Would-be heroes stormed into California. Once Sloat learned of the U.S. declaration of war against Mexico and the subsequent blockade of Veracruz on June 7, he and eight ships of the Pacific Squadron

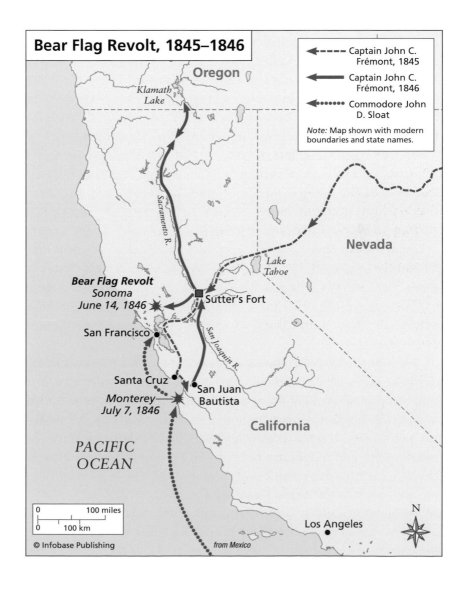

sailed for Monterey, California, without even waiting for orders from Washington. On July 7, 270 U.S. sailors and marines landed and raised a U.S. flag while warships fired a 21-gun salute. On July 9, 1846, Sloat proclaimed California a U.S. territory. In general, the Mexicans felt better about Sloat's relatively ordered, "professional" command than about the unruly Bear Flaggers. But nothing—especially reports of battles in northeast Mexico—convinced California's feuding Mexican governors Castro and Pío Pico that a changeover to U.S. authority would be peaceful or ordered, and they fled south.

Unfortunately, Sloat's poor health resulted in his sudden retirement, and on July 23, 1846, Sloat's colleague, commander of the ship *Congress,* Commodore Robert Stockton, arrived to take his place. Though he had received the same instructions as those given Frémont—keep an eye on the British and encourage Californians to welcome a U.S. takeover of California—Stockton was lacking in tact. He openly declared that Monterey and San Francisco were taken as revenge for Mexico's misdeeds on the Rio Grande and against Frémont. Then Stockton bragged that he would take the rest of California. He established the "California Battalion," consisting of Frémont and the Bear Flaggers, and immediately sent this force south to San Diego to stop any Mexicans trying to reach the border.

By mid-August, forces under Stockton, Frémont, and a marine lieutenant, Archibald Gillespie, entered Los Angeles. Meeting little resistance, on August 17, 1846, they declared the United States in charge of the whole province. But Gillespie, assigned to govern there, had no regard for the Mexican-Californians themselves and was soon overthrown. Not until January 10, 1847, was Los Angeles recaptured by U.S. forces.

Though late, help for the reconquest came in the person of Brig. Gen. Stephen Watts Kearny and his "Army of the West," ordered in May 1846 to march from Fort Levenworth, Kansas, into Santa Fe. On June 3, just before Kearny left, he received "top secret" orders. After conquering the Mexican state of New Mexico, these orders read, he was to keep going and conquer California. The navy, he was assured, would be there in California's ports, ready to help him. The important thing was to enter Alto California before winter.

Although facing a long journey, Kearny and his army would hardly be the first to make this trip west for, since the 1830s, a quite profitable enterprise had developed along this route. In 1821, the

THE EXTRAORDINARY CAREER OF ROBERT STOCKTON

A naval hero of the War of 1812 and in the war against the Barbary pirates, Commodore Robert F. Stockton (1795–1866) was one of the more flamboyant figures who was allowed to pretty much go his own way in the Mexican War. In 1821, he had helped to establish Liberia as a refuge for freed slaves—with force, some say. In the 1830s, his Delaware and Raritan Canal Company made him rich. Stockton supervised construction of the navy's first screw-propeller driven warship in 1844, and in a demonstration for President Tyler, a new cannon aboard exploded, killing several cabinet members, crew, and Tyler's father-in-law. Government inquiry absolved Stockton, and in 1845 he sailed to Texas bearing the U.S. declaration of annexation. Moving on to California in the aftermath of the Bear Flag rebellion, Stockton virtually seized control of California and duped Mexican Californians, claiming that the Yankee rule was "temporary" pending a stable government. He then defied President Polk by assigning the California governorship to "Bear Flagger" John C. Frémont rather than to Polk's candidate, Gen. Stephen Kearny. Commodore William Branford Shubrick replaced Stockton two weeks later, and all California heaved a sigh of relief. Stockton ended his public service as a U.S. senator from New Jersey, serving from 1851 to 1853.

Robert F. Stockton (1795–1866)
(Library of Congress)

William Becknell, Thomas James, and the Glenn-Fowler expedition opened up the legendary Santa Fe Trail to the silver trade. This famous trade route stretched from Independence, Missouri, to the town of Santa Fe, capital of the Mexican state of New Mexico. There Anglo traders and a large Mexican merchant class grew fat. But the poor Mexican farmers (peons) of the area, on the other hand, gained little from commerce brought by the trail. With the Indians, they formed a discontented minority with no love for either Mexican or Anglo-American heroes. Moreover, Texans themselves invaded the territory several times, and New Mexicans and Texans both thought of the other as enemy.

And so, precisely as Sloat and Frémont were claiming Northern California, General Kearny trudged westward with his First Dragoons (the Army of the West). They set out on June 26, 1846. In timely fash-

THE SANTA FE TRAIL

Before Mexico's independence, New Mexico's road system was virtually nonexistent, and *estrangeros* (foreigners) venturing into the territory were often held up or arrested. After 1821, border restrictions eased, and trade started up between the United States and Mexico. The trader William Becknell is credited as being the first to travel the trail to Santa Fe—then part of Mexico—and U.S. traders soon followed as they made their way from Independence, Missouri. Originally a mere path for people and their mules or horses, by 1825 the route was marked, smoothed out, and christened the Santa Fe Trail.

When travelers crossed the Arkansas River near Cimarron, Kansas, they had two possible routes. One led directly across the Cimarron Desert. Although shorter, it exposed travelers to possible attacks by Indians. The other route led along the Arkansas River to Bent's Fort in southeastern Colorado. Established there by the Bent brothers and their partner Ceran St. Vrain, this trading post thrived on the trail's traffic and monopolized trade with the Native Americans. Travelers along this trail would then proceed across the Raton Pass and on to rough-and-ready Taos, New Mexico, continue to nearby Santa Fe, also a rowdy place, and then head south on El Camino Real ("the Royal Highway") to Chihuahua. It was a tough trip, and those who dared make it encountered Indian attacks and physical deprivation. Most did not go without escort.

In reverse, Manuel Armijo, off and on from 1837 to 1844 the Spanish governor of New Mexico, sent his trading caravans to Missouri via the trail. Prosperous Mexican traders sent their children along the trail to Missouri parochial schools and, as apprentices, to St. Louis business houses. However, it was mostly the North American

ion that August, Kearny captured the settlement of Las Vegas, in the Mexican state (and present-day U.S. state) of New Mexico.

There, legend says, he climbed up on a roof to promise the conquered citizens that they would no longer need to fear the marauding Kiowa and Comanche Indians. Kearny and the United States would protect them. And at that moment, he got the whole crowd to swear a loyalty oath to the United States, since they would otherwise be considered traitors.

As Kearny marched on toward Santa Fe, the Mexican resistance under one General Armijo assembled at the narrow Apache Pass, the

merchants who grew rich from the trade in such goods as hardware, knives, clothing, linens and textiles, gold, and beaver skins. A brisk trade also grew up supplying and caring for the caravans themselves. In 1872, as construction of the Santa Fe railway began, the need for the trail was phased out. However, the town of Santa Fe remained a hub in the Southwest.

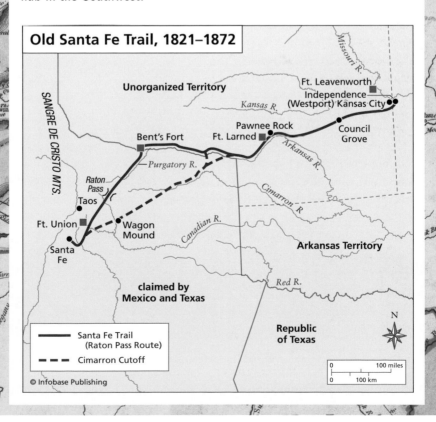

Old Santa Fe Trail, 1821–1872

only route into the city. Something in the way the *norteamericanos* carried themselves as they rode through disturbed Armijo, for he began quarreling with his other officers and finally ordered their troop to disband. Cynics have suggested that Armijo's indifference may have been because he accepted a bribe from Washington. (He left hurriedly as soon as Kearny entered the city.) Whatever the reasons, Armijo's inaction allowed Kearny to march triumphantly into the capital without firing a single round of ammunition.

In Santa Fe, the ambitious Kearny wrote a constitution for New Mexico. Two lawyers in his army, Pvt. Willard Hall and Col. Alexander Doniphan, assisted him. Furious, some members of Congress later pointed out that Kearny had no right either to make laws or grant citizenship. Much of the constitution he wrote, however, remains in force.

On September 25, 1846, confident that Washington was solidly behind him, Kearny began the march to California. In order to do this, he had divided his army—with a total of 1,700 men—into three parts.

The Church of San Miguel, one of the oldest (1636) religious buildings in the United States, is located in Santa Fe, the capital of Mexico's state of New Mexico when General Kearny captured it in August 1846. *(Library of Congress)*

Three hundred dragoons and two howitzers went west with Kearny. Under Col. Sterling Price, another force remained to occupy Santa Fe. A third unit was assigned to subdue the Native Americans and then head south to Chihuahua, southeast of El Paso along the Rio Grande. According to the strategy developed by Scott and Polk in Washington back in May, Santa Fe and Chihuahua were part of the "northern provinces" that the Army of the Center, under General Wool, was to hold "until peace was made."

The third group of soldiers was commanded by Kearny's lawyer friend, Colonel Doniphan, and the first thing he did was to leave for Navajo and Ute territory, the continental watershed between the Rio Grande and the Colorado. At Ojo Oso, or Bear Spring, Doniphan persuaded the Navajo to make a treaty with both the "old" Spanish-speaking New Mexican invaders and the "new" invaders, the Anglos. The treaty was signed on November 22, 1846, and sealed with several beautiful Navajo blankets as gifts. Doniphan sent these to Washington.

The U.S. troops left behind in New Mexico, meanwhile, behaved less than admirably in the winter of 1846–47. They drank, brawled, and mistreated both Mexicans and Indians. The U.S.-appointed governor Charles Bent called the people of New Mexico "mongrels," and evidently organized an elaborate spy system to govern them. "The Americans say they have come for our good," said one irate citizen. "Yes, for all our goods." The poorest of the citizenry suffered the most. Finally, on January 19, 1847, a revolt broke out in Taos. Led by Pablo Montoya, a Mexican peasant, and Tomasito Romero, a Pueblo Indian, the rebels killed Governor Bent and five other *estadosunidenses*. A mob dragged Bent's mangled body through the streets, then destroyed deeds and documents related to land-grabbing schemes of the North Americans.

The Taos Rebellion lasted less than two weeks, but at least 14 more Anglo-Americans were killed. On February 3, Colonel Price and five companies battered a hole in the adobe wall of Taos Pueblo. By nighttime, February 4, Price's troops had killed 150 New Mexicans, executed 25 to 30 prisoners by firing squad, and flogged many who surrendered. The rebellion was over; and the rule of Colonel Price afterward was harsh. U.S. troops would not leave the area until 1851, almost four years after the end of the U.S.-Mexican War.

After concluding the treaty with the Navajo at Bear Spring, Colonel Doniphan and his troops left Santa Fe in November 1846, with 856 men and 315 wagons driven by traders and camp followers. Doniphan was

The Taos Pueblo in New Mexico, where for two weeks in January–February 1847 Indians conducted a rebellion against the U.S. government until U.S. troops brutally suppressed it *(Library of Congress)*

one of the most colorful, though brutal, characters to take part in the war against Mexico. Although neither he nor his troops helped conquer California, after reaching Chihuahua, their subsequent journey to try to join Taylor became one of the legends of its time. Doniphan was enormous, with blazing red hair and hazel eyes. He swore like a sailor and lived like a cowboy alone on the range, cooking for himself and pitching his own tent.

Doniphan's troops, who called themselves the "Ring-tailed Roarers," came from the backwoods. Their first encounter occurred near El Paso, where the greatly outnumbered Americans—coming out of the desert after three days without water—defeated the Mexicans. The Taos Rebellion cut off their supplies, but these unruly fighters were accustomed to living off the places they passed through. Hard as nails, they crossed deserts without shoes and slept through freezing nights after their tents had blown away.

At the end of February 1847, Doniphan and his troops approached Chihuahua. Waiting for them were some 2,700 Mexican soldiers and another 1,000 rancheros with machetes. But just as in the first battle of Palo Alto and Resaca de Palma, Mexican powder was inferior, and their firepower was not much better. It is said that the Anglo troops just dodged when Mexican cannonballs came their way.

The Roarers' artillery, on the other hand, was deadly. Through it all, Doniphan whittled. Reportedly, he punctuated the noise of battle with the remark, "Well, they're giving us hell now, boys." When the defending troops broke for cover, Doniphan's troops attacked. By five o'clock they had killed 300 Mexicans and wounded many more; as for the Roarers, only one was killed and five wounded. They took over Chihuahua, and throughout March Doniphan's troops simply helped themselves to whatever they felt like until 30 percent were unfit for duty.

In April 1847, General Taylor ordered Doniphan to join his forces at Saltillo. To the relief of the Mexicans in Chihuahua, Doniphan left. It was not until he arrived at Taylor's headquarters in Monterrey, some 60 miles northeast of Saltillo, that he met "Old Rough and Ready," who sent Doniphan and his troops back to Missouri. In the year since they had left Missouri, Doniphan and his men had covered more than 6,000 miles and survived against all odds—bad weather, no pay, no supplies. It was the stuff of which epics are made, except that Doniphan's force left a trail of atrocities behind him that only complicated the efforts of Taylor and other Americans in their dealings with Mexicans.

On February 28, 1847, Colonel Doniphan led his volunteers to victory in a battle at the Río Sacramento and then captured the nearby Mexican city of Chihuahua. *(Library of Congress)*

Doniphan's brawling fighters were not the only ones to travel long and hard in this war. In the campaign to take California, and literally to pave the way for Kearny's westward advance, Capt. Philip St. George Cooke led a battalion of Mormons on one of the most difficult forced marches in military history. Mormons were rather despised at that time in U.S. history, but they had just recently (1844) begun to settle Utah under the leadership of Brigham Young, and they favored the U.S.-Mexican War because it meant that Zion (their "promised land" in Utah) would be in the United States rather than in Mexico.

From the original 500, Cooke dismissed the old and infirm until he was down to 397 men. The Mormons' leader, Brigham Young, came personally to bless them and promised that no one would die at the hands of the Mexicans—their special Mormon underwear would protect them, he promised. The unit was to accompany Kearny as a supply train and cut a road through the mountains, from Santa Fe to San Diego, thus linking California to the United States. Anxious to get to California, however, and not sure exactly when the battalion would arrive, Kearny went ahead. The Mormon battalion was to follow, bettering the trail as it went.

On October 6, 1846, as Kearny and his band approached the village of Socorro on the Rio Grande, they met up with a group of bearded and

Christopher (Kit) Carson (1809–68)
(Library of Congress)

dusty frontiersmen led by a man with flowing blond hair. It was Kit Carson, the famous "mountain man" who had guided John Frémont, "the Pathfinder," through the wilderness of the western territories. Carson had been sent by Commodore Stockton with messages to take all the way to Washington to inform the government about events in California. When Kearny learned that the Bear Flaggers and the navy had already won California, he sent back 200 of his 300 dragoons and persuaded Kit—he could not say no—to turn back and serve as guide for the rest of the westward journey. Kearny regarded himself as the new military governor of California, and so he felt his authority superseded Stockton's.

With Carson and several Native American scouts, Kearny headed south along the Rio Grande, then west along the Gila River. By November 22, Kearny and his company reached the point where the Gila meets the Colorado, almost due east of San Diego. The Mormons were trailing behind. Then Kearny encountered a party of Californian horsemen who bore news that California was far from secure. There had been an uprising against the *norteamericanos* under Gillespie in Los Angeles, and San Diego was the only town in southern California still clearly held by the United States.

Not knowing what else to do, Kearny continued into California and reached Agua Caliente on December 2. Forty miles southeast of Los Angeles, on December 6, 1846, Kearny ran smack into a Mexican force led by Andres Pico, brother of the former Mexican governor of California. In the ensuing battle at San Pascual, hand-to-hand combat left 22 U.S. soldiers dead and 16 wounded. The Mexicans counted only two dead, but because they failed to pursue their advantage, neither side really came out victorious. Finally, on December 11, a wearied and slightly wounded Kearny was met by 180 marines (sent by Stockton) and escorted into San Diego.

Although the two men did not get on especially well, Kearny and Stockton's forces did combine in the final battle to retake Los Angeles. There, when they faced the Mexican force at the San Gabriel River, the Americans charged, and at least one report claims that the Mexicans simply turned and ran. On January 10, 1847, the U.S. forces retook Los Angeles, and from that point on California was effectively a U.S. territory.

Before returning to his fleet, Stockton had appointed Frémont to be governor of California, but Kearny was sure that he had been empowered by Washington to hold that position. Frémont refused to step aside, so in March Kearny arrested him and sent him back to Washington to be court-martialed. He was found guilty, but President Polk remitted any penalty. Frémont resigned from the army, returned to California as a civilian, and eventually became one of California's first senators when it joined the Union.

The story of the California campaign cannot be closed until the Mormon battalion is accounted for. They did not even get away from Santa Fe until October 19, some two weeks after Kearny had already met up with Kit Carson, and their journey turned into yet another epic trek. Although they did not have to fight either Mexicans or Indians, they had a horrendously difficult passage across the craggy Sacramento range of New Mexico and then across the deserts of southern Arizona and California. For three days and two nights, they had no water and nearly ran out of rations. To get through a narrow canyon that brought them into California, they had to take each wagon completely apart, go through the pass and reassemble all of them on the other side. It was January 29, 1847, before they arrived at San Diego, and Captain Cooke would write: "Marching half naked and half fed, and living upon wild animals, we have discovered and made a road of great value to our country . . . History may be searched in vain for an equal march of infantry." This wagon road, known as the Gila Trail, would soon be a route for those seeking their fortune in the California gold rush of 1849.

The discoveries that started that gold rush were made near the very Sutter's Fort where Frémont and his Bear Flaggers had begun the revolt against the Mexicans. So Polk's dream of reaping the benefits of California would pay off quickly. But long before this, and while the struggle for California and the Southwest was still in full swing, the war in northeast and central Mexico was proceeding in deadly earnest.

"MR. POLK'S WAR"

On September 25, 1846—about the same time that Lieutenant Gillespie was about to raise a flag of truce and turn Los Angeles back to the Mexicans—the Mexican flag came down over Monterrey in Tamaulipas state and Gen. Zachary Taylor and his troops raised the U.S. flag. Mexican troops filed gloomily out of Monterrey and U.S. forces marched in to the tune of shrill piccolos playing "Yankee Doodle." General Taylor agreed to let the defeated General Ampudia retreat with arms because he believed Ampudia's plea that the Mexicans needed guns to defend themselves against the Comanche and the Kiowa, Native American tribes of the area. Taylor also promised not to advance farther into Mexico for eight weeks.

As soon as President Polk heard of Taylor's victory and the terms of the ceasefire, he was furious. From the outset, he and his cabinet had conceived of a quick, decisive victory against Mexico, and Polk was sure that the long peace would only give the Mexicans more time to prepare for the next battle.

Indeed, armchair strategists in Washington had an entirely different campaign in mind than the one Taylor was conducting. First, William Learned Marcy, Polk's secretary of war, planned an invasion of Tampico, the port city of the Mexican state of Tamaulipas, located halfway between Matamoros and Veracruz along Mexico's Gulf Coast. From there, the plan was to take Veracruz. On September 23, as the battle at Monterrey raged, Marcy wrote to Commodore David Conner, naval commander at Brazos, at the mouth of the Rio Grande, asking the commodore to take Tampico. Marcy then sent a message to Taylor to send several of his units to help him.

The messages to Taylor and to Conner were intercepted by the Mexicans. Learning that the small Gulf port of Tampico was about to be invaded, the town's local commander, Gen. Anastasio Parrodi, sent all the town's valuable munitions up the Panuco River, through the

On September 24, 1846, after the five-day siege and battle for Monterrey, General Ampudia (at left) formally surrendered to General Taylor. *(Library of Congress)*

pass at Tula to Santa Anna's secret headquarters at San Luis Potosí, a silver-mining town a little more than 200 miles due south of Monterrey and about 200 miles west of the seaport.

Taylor knew nothing about the activities of Santa Anna, who was busy gathering together his Army of Liberation at San Luis Potosí. Nor was he aware of the initial orders regarding the taking of Tampico. Not until October 10, 1846, did official word of the proposed invasion of Tampico reach Taylor's headquarters. (Ironically, Taylor's official announcement of the victory at Monterrey and about the eight-week armistice—sent on September 25—did not arrive in Washington until October 11.)

Taylor was livid. He fired off a dispatch, telling the War Department that he had the right to organize his own campaign. Unfortunately, Washington knew nothing of the intercepted messages and when the War Department actually received Taylor's dispatch on time, Taylor appeared to be disobeying orders.

The end result was that Polk ordered Taylor and a small force to stay in Monterrey and defend it. But Taylor thought that instead he could occupy Saltillo and force the Mexicans to wage an offensive war. He had already ordered one of his subordinates, Gen. William

J. Worth, to go ahead of him and subdue Saltillo. On November 13, essentially in defiance of Polk's orders, Taylor left Monterrey and headed southwest for Saltillo with some 5,000 men to complete the taking of that city.

Taylor did not know that on the very next day, November 14, Commodore Conner fulfilled his orders by occupying a quiet Tampico (whose arms and munitions had disappeared upriver to Santa Anna's hideaway in San Luis Potosí). Nor did Taylor know that Conner would order one of his junior officers, Captain Perry, to go north up the coast to the mouth of the Rio Grande to help divert U.S. troops—coming in to serve with Taylor—to the Veracruz campaign.

In Washington, Taylor's rival, Gen. Winfield Scott, badly wanted to get out of the capital and lead the Veracruz expedition himself. Back on October 27, in his earliest memorandum, entitled "Veracruz and its castle," Scott proposed a strategy for going all the way from Veracruz to Mexico City, and when he later put this strategy into action, it would make Scott famous. Polk, however, was reluctant to give Scott the assignment.

On November 12, Scott sent Polk another memo. This one described the winning formula. Tamaulipas and north central Mexico were secure; now, no less than 10,000 fresh troops from the United

The valley toward Saltillo, looking southwest from Monterrey (*Library of Congress*)

States were to be put on boats at New Orleans no later than January 1, 1847. Twenty thousand more troops from those already in Mexico or on the way to Matamoros were to be added. Everyone was to be gathered at Brazos and, from there, sent to Veracruz, which they would capture, and from there, move west, inland, to Mexico City. So long as the inland journey began before May, yellow fever season, the plan would work.

Although Scott's plan was well-reasoned and sensible, Polk did not want to use Scott to head such an expedition. But there he was, General Scott, at 60, a huge man—six foot four—with fly-away clumps of whiskers on either side of his face called "muttonchops." A War of 1812 hero, he was a Whig with possible presidential ambitions. Scott was arrogant but charismatic; he loved the brass and polish of military show, and he insisted on discipline. There would be no more atrocities from the Texas Rangers or Doniphan's wild men under Scott.

Indeed, many felt that Polk was overly sensitive about Scott. Who else could lead the army on to Mexico City? Angry with Taylor for the

Maj. Gen. Winfield Scott (1786–1866), here depicted after his capture of Veracruz, would lead his troops to the final victory in Mexico City five and a half months later. *(Library of Congress)*

MEXICAN VERSUS NORTH AMERICAN MILITARY STRATEGY

The U.S.-Mexican War was the first that the United States fought entirely on foreign territory, and military strategists regard it as a military milestone. The initial plan was to blockade the coast of Mexico and occupy the northern Mexican states: Mexico was supposed to go belly up and ask for negotiations. It emphatically did not.

Strategy was then altered to seek victory in central Mexico, as Scott entered the fray via Veracruz on Mexico's Gulf coast. Scott's strategy at Veracruz—the equivalent of carpet bombing instead of pitting soldier against soldier, away from civilians—shocked the international community. Although he had discovered Scott's plans, Santa Anna made a strategic blunder in trying to defeat Taylor at Buena Vista in the north before turning to fight off Scott farther to the southeast. Cavalry and artillery were the key to offensive action (thus Scott's important realization of the value of light artillery for maximum maneuverability).

Although Scott was delayed at Puebla, waiting for reinforcements, Santa Anna, having been humiliated at Cerro Gordo, did nothing. His strategy collapsed, and the Mexicans would never again seize the offense throughout the war. In August, Scott methodically drove Mexican troops back toward Mexico City, defeat after defeat, until he won at Chapultepec.

Ironically, both Santa Anna and General Scott admired Napoleonic military strategy. Santa Anna used French tactics at Buena Vista, trying to overwhelm American positions with dense columns of troops, but tier upon tier of infantry and artillery repelled them. Indeed one of Santa Anna's strategic flaws was to use men like cannon fodder. North American forces were more pragmatic, whereas Santa Anna seemed to lack the ability to change his plans when the tide of battle changed.

Near the end of the war, desperate Mexicans resorted to guerrilla forays against the U.S. line of communications as Scott moved on Mexico City. They sought to imitate the old Spanish tactics against Napoléon and then the methods used to win their own independence from Spain in 1821. But they were disheartened, and their attempts degenerated into banditry. Only when General Taylor dispatched reinforcements, especially the Texas Rangers under John Coffee Hays, were communications reopened and the guerrilla attacks reduced.

armistice at Monterrey and having asked Taylor to give up troops to support a Veracruz invasion, Polk could hardly ask "Old Rough-and-Ready" to lead the United States on to Mexico City.

On November 16, Taylor occupied Saltillo without any opposition. But his real object was Victoria, the inland capital of Tamaulipas. For he had finally heard rumors of Santa Anna's preparations at San Luis Potosí, and Victoria, Taylor thought, "threatens the flank of the Mexican army should it advance from San Luis."

On November 18, President Polk, with his cabinet concurring, finally said "yes" to Scott's plea for appointment as commander of the Mexico City campaign. On November 25, Scott sent a very polite letter to Taylor requesting that Taylor give up some of his "gallant officers and men" for an unnamed campaign along the Gulf. He hoped to make short work of this war with the use of Taylor's regulars that he requested and some good volunteers.

A damaged but still fascinating daguerreotype (an early form of photography) shows the occupation of Saltillo, November 1847. Volunteers of the Virginia Regiment are on parade. *(Courtesy Beinecke Rare Book and Manuscript Library, Yale University)*

At the same time that November, Polk's opposition, the Whigs, won the House of Representatives. One of the major campaign issues had been the unpopular and, in the opinion of many, unnecessary war that Polk had initiated with Mexico. Campaign slogans sneered, "Mr. Polk's War!" The political situation, as well as the military one, was full of drama, and the Whig victory meant that no lawmaker and not even the general public would support a long, drawn-out campaign. A great deal of Polk's hopes were pinned on Scott's speedy success.

By then, in fact, Scott was busily preparing to go to Mexico. On November 30, he took a boat to New Orleans, intending to go from there to Tampico. In those days, the sleek and speedy clipper ship was the means of travel. But it was still a sailing ship, and wind was both enemy and friend to it. Nevertheless, no one would have predicted that head winds would delay Scott's arrival in New Orleans for three weeks.

Nor could anyone predict that Polk would astonish and enrage Congress by trying to give an old political crony, Senator Thomas Hart Benton, the job of lieutenant general responsible for movements in northern Mexico. That would make Benton Taylor's superior, overseer of the attack on the capital from Veracruz, and supervisor of negotiations for peace. Benton was totally unqualified. With alarm at the president's poor judgment, the Senate tabled the measure. Polk's maneuver nearly sabotaged the whole Mexico City campaign and kept Scott waiting in New Orleans for orders which had been slowed by the wrangling in Congress.

Two days after Christmas, Scott arrived at Brazos, at the mouth of the Rio Grande. Not finding Taylor there to greet him, Scott asked one of Taylor's officers to select which units, among those allotted to Taylor, would go to Veracruz. Troops came from all over, including the continental United States, which provided nine new volunteer regiments. Among many other supplies, Scott requested that all ships coming to Mexico bring 60 days' worth of firewood and enough Mississippi River water in casks to supply crews at Brazos and Tampico as well as the invading force.

At the same time, Santa Anna and his troops were pouring into San Luis Potosí to the southwest. After nearly a month's delay in the supply line, Taylor left a small force at Saltillo, and, on December 13, began the march to Victoria. Thus, he missed Scott's letters. But Taylor's intelligence got wind of Santa Anna's movements: Santa Anna sneaked an attack on Saltillo and Taylor had to double back to protect his forces.

An even smaller unit commanded by Taylor's officer, Brigadier General Quitman, continued on to Victoria and took it without resistance on December 29.

Taylor continued northward back toward Monterrey. While he was engaged in this movement, on January 25, 1847, the *New York Express* published a letter Taylor had written back in early November claiming that he could win the war by staying at Saltillo and forcing the Mexicans to expend large numbers of men and resources into repeated attacks. Clearly, Taylor's was not the strategy the administration had in mind. With the publication of Taylor's letter, Polk's patience with his general was done. Polk publicly scolded Taylor and assigned Winfield Scott as not only the director of the Veracruz–Mexico City expedition but also supreme commander of the whole war. Instructions were drafted to Taylor and the dispatch was sent. Mistakenly included was the list of all units earmarked for Scott's Veracruz invasion.

Another daguerreotype shows Gen. John E. Wool *(left of center)* and his staff arriving in Saltillo to reinforce General Taylor prior to the Battle of Buena Vista. *(Courtesy Beinecke Rare Book and Manuscript Library, Yale University)*

On January 30, 1847, by then headquartered at Monterrey, Taylor moved his force out to Saltillo once more. After reaching Saltillo on February 2, he decided to go even farther south and moved 18 more miles to Agua Nueva because he thought such a move would spare Saltillo and cut off the Mexicans from their water and valuable supplies. This move also brought Taylor closer to a confrontation with the Mexicans, who were heading north toward Monterrey.

Santa Anna trotted in front of his troops as they wound their way through the barren hills from San Luis Potosí to Monterrey. This was the new Army of Liberation, the 18,000 that would finally rid Mexico of the hated *norteamericanos.* Then a dust cloud lingered a little way off to one side of the long line of troops. It grew larger, then revealed a Mexican soldier in a sombrero who rode out of the dust on a horse with a silver-studded bridle. The rider's musket was still in its sling on the side of his saddle, yet he waved a piece of paper over his head with as much excitement as if he were leading a charge on the enemy.

Mexican spies had scored again: They had caught the U.S. messenger with a lariat, killing him, and they had found the message containing the list of the units the U.S. Army would use to invade Veracruz. A huge chunk of Taylor's army, it seemed, would be in Veracruz. Santa Anna reasoned, wrongly, that Taylor's force at Agua Nueva was just another group of reinforcements going to help Scott. Why not finish them off, he reasoned, instead of letting Taylor send them to help conquer Mexico City?

Foolishly, Santa Anna now decided to push his green recruits 45 miles in less than 24 hours to wage a surprise attack on Taylor. No food, no rest. Then battle. But the decision to engage Taylor at this point was the wrong one on Santa Anna's part. Gathering together the new Army of Liberation had not been as easy or as glamorous as he had boasted it would be. Supplies were low and money to support the war effort had been slow in coming. While Santa Anna had created a huge army—not the 25,000 he bragged about, but a good 18,000—at least half of them had never seen a battle before. They knew nothing of the strategies of war that Santa Anna used—most of them had never heard of the famous French general Napoléon Bonaparte, whose tactics were so admired by the general. In the seven or eight weeks before Scott landed at Veracruz, Santa Anna might have gotten his men in shape to beat the *norteamericanos.* And if that landing had been defeated, Mexico City would be safe. So would Mexico.

Gen. John E. Wool (1784–1869) along with Gen. Zachary Taylor, commanded the U.S. forces in their successful two-day battle at Buena Vista, February 22–23, 1847. *(Library of Congress)*

Meanwhile, in a little town called Enchanted (La Encantada), Taylor conferred with Gen. John Wool. They were about 20 miles south of Saltillo with a combined force of only 4,800 troops because, after dutifully responding to Polk's orders, Taylor had finally sent the requested units to Scott for his invasion of Veracruz. Suddenly,

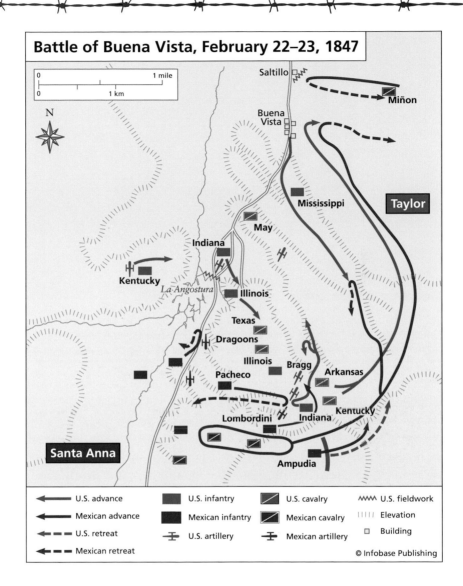

Battle of Buena Vista, February 22–23, 1847

John Wool, ordinarily the most gentlemanly of soldiers, was heard shouting. He was annoyed at the news that the foe, according to U.S. scouts, far outnumbered them—a force of 18,000. Now Taylor wanted to stay put, and Wool wanted to go on to a more strategic position.

There was more talk, then Wool and Taylor called their aides. The orders spread through the ranks—they were to move 10 miles farther, to a hacienda called San Juan de la Buena Vista at La Angostura, or "The Narrows."

In a once famous incident before the Battle of Buena Vista, when General Santa Anna is said to have demanded that the U.S. forces surrender, General Taylor proclaimed, "General Taylor never surrenders!" *(Library of Congress)*

The two men took their separate positions in the territory between Buena Vista and Saltillo. Wool, on horseback, went over and over the Buena Vista territory, until finally he came up with an idea. The road at Buena Vista went through steep mountains. Gullies and ravines fell away to either side and at one point the mountains came nearly to the roadside. On every long, high plateau, Wool posted soldiers and most of the 15 guns in their possession. Wool sent men scurrying everywhere, then called his cavalry. To make the road even more difficult for the Mexicans, Wool emptied wagonload after wagonload of boulders onto the road, blocking it. Taylor acknowledged that Wool's choice of Buena Vista was a good one. They were going to need all the help they could get.

After their labors, the soldiers took a brief rest. For a moment, they just watched as the Mexicans began to arrive. Santa Anna's proud but inexperienced army started forward, then backed up, then huddled with their regiment leaders. The canyon was simply too narrow to accommodate more than half of Santa Anna's troops. Cavalry whirled, horses reared, then cantered off and back to look once more.

Then, under Gen. Juan Minon, 2,500 of Santa Anna's cavalry rode off in a wide circle to threaten Taylor's position nearer Saltillo. Other

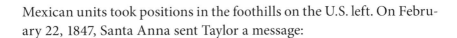
Mexican units took positions in the foothills on the U.S. left. On February 22, 1847, Santa Anna sent Taylor a message:

> You are surrounded by twenty thousand men, and cannot avoid being cut to pieces. I wish to save you this disaster, and summon you to surrender at your discretion and give you an hour to make up your mind.

But, unmoved by Santa Anna's ultimatum, Taylor decided to do battle. He took full advantage of the rough terrain, with its deep ravines and high defensive ground. Santa Anna was not so clever, it seemed, and planned a battle more suitable for an open field: By dividing his army into three weak units, he failed to capitalize on his numerical advantage.

When Santa Anna launched a massive attack through the ravines, U.S. artillerymen fired furiously, the metal shot like machine-gun fire cutting them down by the hundreds. Reportedly, gunners mixed the stones at their feet in with the ammunition, and that had two effects. One was to give an even denser shot. The other was to make the metal scatter over a wider arc. Santa Anna nearly broke the line, however, by sheer numbers.

Gen. Zachary Taylor is depicted here looking through a telescope as he commands U.S. troops in the Battle of Buena Vista. *(Library of Congress)*

On the second day of the fighting at Buena Vista, Kentuckian cavalry made a gallant charge that helped to turn the battle in favor of the U.S. forces. *(Library of Congress)*

In another corner, young Jefferson Davis led a flamboyantly dressed unit of volunteers who, in their inexperience could not form a phalanx—a customary military formation in the shape of a square. That is what the more professional Mexican officer was prepared for, but instead the Yanks lured their attackers into a wide V and then caught them and their beautiful horses in the crossfire. The animals fell, shot at the knees, whinnying as their riders plunged to the ground and looked up to the Mississippi rangers baring 18-inch bowie knives.

Still, at the end of the first day of fighting, Taylor's chief of staff, William Wallace Smith Bliss, reported that the majority of Taylor's army was "entirely demoralized. The commander of the Illinois volunteers had been killed, along with Henry Clay, the son of the senator; Colonel Archibald McKee; and the commander of the Second Kentucky Volunteers, Archibald Yell." He went on to tally the dead and added glumly that Jefferson Davis, "the best volunteer field officer in the army," was wounded and delirious, "leaving the Mississippi helpless."

Yet the next day, Maj. Braxton Bragg overwhelmed the Mexicans with more of the superior U.S. artillery fire. At every attack, the Mexi-

TRAINING GROUND FOR THE CIVIL WAR

Differences regarding expansion, slavery, and the Union flourished in the fertile ground of the U.S.-Mexican War and helped fan the fires of the Civil War. Further, the war with Mexico was the first one in which more than a handful of West Point–trained officers were engaged, and it gave both Northern and Southern soldiers, especially officers, practice in waging war. It perpetuated certain wartime beliefs and practices, including the prohibition against using black Americans as soldiers. Although in the Civil War, the Union army would change that, Robert Gould Shaw's black regiment would have been unthinkable in the Mexican War. Indeed, a manual was issued to help U.S. doctors in the Mexican War detect "Negro blood" in recruits.

Although the Civil War was between peers and the Mexican War was one of conquest, many of both wars' recruits were excited by the glory of war, the sense that "God is on our side," and revenge for previous losses. In both conflicts, the officers tended to look down on ordinary recruits. Recruits' racist views of Mexicans made conquest easier for them; similarly, in the Civil War many recruits held negative views of their enemy. As the Civil War wore on, this changed, however, and numerous reports exist of Confederates and Union soldiers fraternizing between the lines. In that sense, the Mexican War was not at all like the Civil War.

Most telling is the roll call of mature Civil War officers who were veterans of the U.S.-Mexican War, starting with Robert E. Lee and Ulysses S. Grant. Other Civil War leaders who saw service in Mexico included George Meade, George McClellan, Braxton Bragg, William Sherman, Stonewall Jackson. Joseph E. Johnston, P. G. T. Beauregard, and Joseph Hooker. Confederate president Jefferson Davis led the First Mississippi Rifles in the earliest part of the war in Mexico. California troops, known as "the California Column," were Mexican War veterans and saw action during the Civil War as part of the 2nd Massachusetts Cavalry, under the command of Gen. James H. Carleton. In many ways, then, the U.S.-Mexican War was literally a training exercise for the Civil War.

cans were narrowly driven back and had to fight their enemy face-to-face. Finally, darkness came just in time to allow the army of Santa Anna to retreat back to San Luis Potosí. Once again, U.S. artillery, marksmanship, and bare knives had outdone him.

Seven hundred U.S. soldiers were dead or wounded; another 1,500 were scattered and had lost the stomach for fighting again. Retreat, retreat, advised Wool, but Taylor's men slept where they had stopped fighting. It was a cold February in the mountains, and the battle had worn them out.

They anticipated that the fight would be renewed in the morning, but no enemy rose to oppose them. Santa Anna had gone. The only fire to be seen was the slow, unwinding smoke of abandoned campfires. Two thousand wounded or dead Mexicans remained behind. And, so the story goes, Taylor and Wool threw their arms about each other and wept. Although he had moved against orders and lost so many men, Taylor had won against huge odds, and the resulting tales of glory made him a hero again.

When the news reached the United States, the impact of victory at Buena Vista was enormous. Though officially antiwar, even the Whigs were stirred by such a victory as Buena Vista, and Taylor began to look very presidential indeed. Polk struggled, rather unsuccessfully, not to say the wrong thing, noting that Taylor disobeyed orders (and might have saved more lives if he had not), but that he owed his success to the bravery of his men.

The Mexicans hung their heads in shame, though Santa Anna brazenly claimed that he had won. Ragged and worn, his troops returned to Mexico City with a few American prisoners he had taken along the way. Santa Anna pointed to these men as proof of his claim. On March 6, 1847, this same claim appeared in *El Locomotor,* the Veracruz newspaper, just as Scott's troops occupied that Gulf seaport. But the men of Santa Anna's army, if not Santa Anna himself, must have known that Buena Vista foreshadowed the fate of their nation in this war.

TAMPICO AND VERACRUZ

General Taylor's stunning victory at Buena Vista still lay several months ahead when, on November 14, 1846, Commodore Conner's landing party arrived at Tampico, one of the stepping-stones on the way to Mexico City, according to the plan devised in Washington by General Scott and President Polk. Most of the civilian inhabitants, terrified of the invaders because of the reputation of the U.S. soldiers, had fled the city, but a small group of unarmed citizens was waiting nervously at Tampico. Even had they known that Taylor had refused to reenlist many of the Texas Rangers because their behavior was so brutal at Monterrey, the Tampicans had heard reports of the equally atrocious behavior of Doniphan's "Ring-tailed Roarers." But Conner assured the citizens of Tampico that their safety and their private property would be protected.

The army settled in for what turned out to be three months of occupation before the February 18, 1847, arrival of Gen. Winfield Scott, high commander and organizer of the campaign to take Mexico City. Meanwhile, by Scott's orders, General Patterson, a political appointee of War Secretary Marcy, took charge of Tampico, and the United States soon transformed the city. Each regiment had a band, and many played in the *zócalo,* or town square; a North American troupe of actors brought "American Theatre" to Anglophile audiences; someone had even started the *Tampico Sentinel,* an English-language newspaper. On the other hand, *pulque,* a mildly fermented drink found in the steamier parts of Mexico, did not satisfy the soldiers used to whiskey, and though Patterson forbade alcohol, the stronger local intoxicants, *mescal* and *aguardiente,* still managed to get into the U.S. troops. Army personnel in Tampico liked to brag that their crime rate was low—not as in Taylor's camps along the Rio Grande—but the atmosphere was far from genteel.

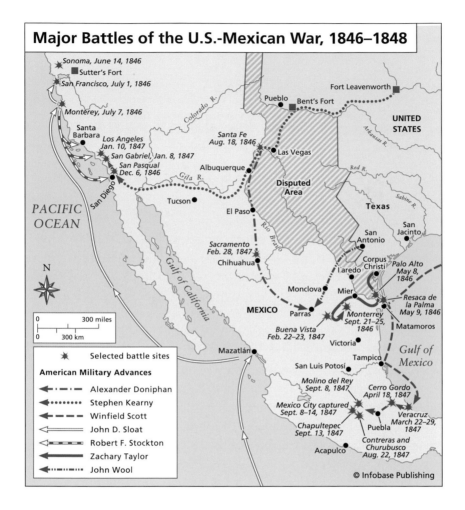

Major Battles of the U.S.-Mexican War, 1846–1848

Sonoma, June 14, 1846
Sutter's Fort
San Francisco, July 1, 1846
Monterey, July 7, 1846
Santa Barbara
Los Angeles Jan. 10, 1847
San Gabriel, Jan. 8, 1847
San Pasqual Dec. 6, 1846
San Diego

PACIFIC OCEAN

N

Fort Leavenworth
Pueblo   Bent's Fort
UNITED STATES
Santa Fe Aug. 18, 1846
Las Vegas
Albuquerque
Disputed Area
Tucson
El Paso
Texas
San Antonio
San Jacinto
Sacramento Feb. 28, 1847
Chihuahua
Corpus Christi
Palo Alto May 8, 1846
Laredo
Monclova   Mier
Resaca de la Palma May 9, 1846
MEXICO   Parras
Monterrey Sept. 21–25, 1846
Matamoros
Buena Vista Feb. 22–23, 1847
Victoria
Mazatlán
Tampico
Gulf of Mexico
San Luis Potosí
Molino del Rey Sept. 8, 1847
Cerro Gordo April 18, 1847
Mexico City captured Sept. 8–14, 1847
Veracruz March 22–29, 1847
Chapultepec Sept. 13, 1847
Puebla
Contreras and Churubusco Aug. 22, 1847
Acapulco

Colorado R.
Arkansas R.
Red R.
Sabine R.
Gila R.
Rio Bravo
Gulf of California

| 0 | | 300 miles |
| 0 | | 300 km |

★   Selected battle sites

American Military Advances

◄–·–·– Alexander Doniphan
◄······· Stephen Kearny
◄– – – Winfield Scott
◄═══ John D. Sloat
◄–■–■– Robert F. Stockton
◄───── Zachary Taylor
◄··–··–·· John Wool

© Infobase Publishing

On February 15, after weeks of delay due to stormy weather and a shortage of ships, Scott and his fleet had set sail from Brazos Santiago at the mouth of the Rio Grande. Finally Scott's expedition—his heavy steamers, swift sailing boats, and cargo—were slipping efficiently through the waters of the Gulf of Mexico. In the same way, Scott expected that none of his recruits would disturb the efficiency of his conquest. His officers were not allowed to get drunk, to gamble, or to chase women. He expected them to be well read and to show some polish. This was a far cry from Taylor, whom Scott later described as having a mind

> . . . that had not been enlarged and refreshed by reading, or much converse with the world. Rigidity of idea was the conse-

quence . . . In short, few men have ever had a more comfortable, labor-saving contempt for learning of every kind.

Yet, despite Scott's reputation as something of a martinet, it is said that he loved his men and often tried to see the world through their eyes. He was concerned enough about his men's welfare, for example, to write an artillery manual that told the gunner how to do absolutely everything, from loading his weapon to cocking the trigger, and even positioning the fingernails when firing.

On February 18, Scott landed at the mouth of the Rio Pánuco in Tampico. It was a relief to see land after a demon wind held them at Brazos for three days and, for three days more, made the ships navigate through choppier water than any landlubber on board was accustomed to. As they neared the riverbank, the men aboard the ships could see a small welcoming party, a little stiff, but with a band playing gallantly at their arrival. Escort troops went through a brief routine as the ships bumped gently into the piers and ropes snaked from hands on deck to hands on shore. Scott's troops filed ashore.

While Tampico did not exactly look like home, there was something familiar about it. For three months, the U.S. Army had been

The Texas Rangers had notorious reputations among Mexican citizens. *(Library of Congress)*

stationed there, and the army camp atmosphere of Tampico was, unfortunately, what seemed so familiar to Scott as he entered town. As he rode through the streets, Scott passed a noisy saloon. A brassy sound spilled into the streets—the Mexican music of a mariachi band. He looked up at the sign that swung over the entrance. *The Rough and Ready Restaurant,* it announced. Scott shuddered in disgust. That did it. On February 19, Scott made a new kind of military history.

He issued General Order No. 20, the same general order he would later reissue at Veracruz, at Puebla, at Mexico City, the order that extended the authority of U.S. military courts in occupied territory. Before, no one had authority to prosecute members of the U.S. Army who committed civilian crimes in an occupied territory. Now, under the Articles of War, if a U.S. soldier should rob, murder, rape, damage private property, or exhibit public drunkenness, the military

The Río Pánuco in Tampico, where Gen. Winfield Scott landed in 1847 *(Library of Congress)*

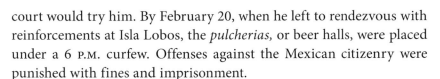

court would try him. By February 20, when he left to rendezvous with reinforcements at Isla Lobos, the *pulcherias,* or beer halls, were placed under a 6 P.M. curfew. Offenses against the Mexican citizenry were punished with fines and imprisonment.

On February 21, 1847, under sunny Caribbean weather, with only a few crests on the waves, Scott's fleet arrived at the next stepping-stone, the Isla Lobos, 60 miles south of Tampico. More ships arrived daily: The Lobos anchorage, said one volunteer, "looked like a wilderness of spars and rigging." It was a motley crew of U.S. forces now rendezvousing there—remnants of a regiment that had been shipwrecked trying to escape a Mexican blockade, the first forces from east of Appalachia, along with the troops Scott had been leading from New Orleans as well as the regular army forces of Taylor he had commandeered at Brazos Santiago. One ship was filled with men who had contracted smallpox while another area was roped off to keep those exposed to the disease quarantined.

By this time, Mexico's military intelligence was aware of plans to take Veracruz, and considering the fact that the U.S. forces were so far from home and Veracruz was so strongly fortified, it might have appeared that Scott's expedition had little chance of success. But Mexico was having its own troubles. With Santa Anna off fighting the North American invaders, in December 1846 the Mexicans had elected as their new president the liberal reformer Valentín Gómez Farías. More than ever, Mexico needed funds. The Mexican troops had only bits and pieces of uniforms, practically no training, and food supplies were inconsistent at best.

Unaware that the United States had sent a secret agent, Moses Beach, to incite dissension among the conservative Mexican clergy, Gómez Farías continued searching for money to fund the war effort. No friend of the wealthy, conservative Roman Catholic Church, Gómez Farías on February 4, 1847, finally persuaded the Mexican congress to pass a law that proclaimed the sale of church property in the amount of 15 million pesos. (At this time, the dollar and the peso were equal in value, so this was a large sum of money.)

When this law passed, the Mexican clergy and many of the conservative elements in Mexico began a protest that within weeks became yet another revolution. But one of the first results was that all four brigades of the Mexican national guard now refused to leave Mexico City for Veracruz. When Gómez Farías ordered them to move out,

CHURCH AND STATE IN MEXICO

Whether purely or partly Indian, Mexican peasants regarded the Catholic Church with ambivalence. From the Conquest on down, they had often suffered at the hands of the Christian missions. In Spain's own Golden Age—a culture that embraced people such as Cervantes, author of *Don Quixote* (1605–15), and Mexican poet Sor Juana (1648–95)—the church brought the Inquisition to Mexico. It acquired huge landholdings; utilized indigenous, then slave, labor; received a generous share of the country's silver and gold; and was supported additionally by tithes imposed on workers and the public. The church's "headquarters" grew fat.

Outlying missions sent to Christianize the Indians of California, New Mexico, and Texas, however, did not enjoy the wealth of their metropolitan centers. Indeed, the rural church provided martyrs to the cause of indigenous peoples. In 1810, a country priest named Father Miguel Hidalgo gave the famous Grito de Dolores, the "Outcry of Dolores" (referring to his town of Dolores), which began the Mexican Revolution and persuaded local Indians to help by rising up against their exploitation. The Revolution's end in 1821 marked the first time that the church was challenged in the Americas. Desperate to raise operating capital, the newly independent republic raided church funds. Neither the church nor the indebted new government of Mexico could provide food or funds to their outlying missions and presidios. The new state's solution—to open Mexican lands to prosperous Anglo settlers—would become fatal to Mexican sovereignty.

they simply refused to obey and, instead, took up defensive positions in the capital. When the government tried to disarm them, on February 27, open fighting broke out. The shooting was haphazard, and a great many *pronunciamentos,* or proclamations, were exchanged back and forth. But nothing was accomplished. The city was crippled by the conflict in which neither the government nor the rebels won anything nor gave in. President Farías was beside himself.

The mutinous soldiers were nicknamed the "Polkos," after their OOM-pa-pa, OOM-pa-pa, OOM-pa-pa music, the polka-like tune that had been adopted for the hymn of the Guardia Nacional, or National Guard (in this case, not like the modern U.S. National Guard, but the

Little changed. In 1847, Mariano Otero, a forward-looking Mexican of the time, noted that the high-ranked clerical minority still lived "surrounded by the greatest abundance." Those of lower rank—the majority—were nearly destitute. The church was the state religion, he noted, and its absolute power was at stake should Mexico lose the war. Not until the Constitution of 1917 was the influence of the church banned: No longer would the Roman Catholic church be the official religion of Mexico. Church and state were finally separated.

The architecture of this church in Juárez is typical of Mexican churches. *(National Archives)*

army itself). They were the most conservative element in Mexican society, many still yearning for a king, for a world of privilege and rank. More than victory over the *norteamericanos,* the guard wanted its political way. And the Mexican government now had a full-blown rebellion on its hands, one that it could not stop easily.

As a consequence, Santa Anna was forced to return to Mexico City from Encarnación, hoping to nip the rebellion in the bud. But, despite Santa Anna's efforts, the Polkos still carried on their revolt against the government. Cadets and conservative military raged in the streets of Mexico City; they raged against the sale of church lands, but they also raged against the humiliation of U.S. presence on their soil. For La

Guerra de la Defensa, "the war of defense" as Mexicans still call the war, was a terrible blow to national pride. Everyone wanted the insult to go away. Instead, Mexican soldiers were staging a rebellion in Mexico City rather than going to defend the port city as enemy troops made their way to Veracruz.

On the day before Scott began bombarding Veracruz—March 21—Santa Anna took the oath and assumed the presidential office, with almost dictatorial powers. Santa Anna immediately applied pressure on the Catholic Church for funds. After the church "volunteered" to give $2 million toward the war effort, he repealed the hated law that was responsible for putting church property up for sale. This accomplished at least two things: It removed the apparent cause of the Polkos Rebellion, and it enabled the Mexican army to respond to the insult of the North Americans' presence. But as furious as they now were, the Mexican army had delayed too long and the siege of Veracruz was by then under way.

On March 2, 1847, a blue, red-centered flag flapped at the main masthead, yardarms creaked, and, with the snap of the canvas, the steamer *Massachusetts* took the lead at the head of Scott's convoy of ships out from Isla Lobos to the naval station of Anton Lizardo, some 12 miles farther on. Steamers and clippers followed. The light wind rose steadily over the next three days until the wind blew at gale force, and off they went, 180 miles south from Anton Lizardo toward Veracruz. Writing to his mother, artilleryman John Vinton reported:

> The weather is delightful, our troops in good health and spirits, and all things look auspicious of success. I am only afraid the Mexicans will not meet us & give us battle—for, to gain everything without controversy after our large & expensive preparations . . . would give us officers no chance for exploits and honors. [Vinton later died during the siege of Veracruz.]

Behind the troop transports, they towed Scott's pride and joy. These were his famous "surf boats," built in sets of three, 40 feet by 12, with bow and stern alike, pointed. Three fit inside one another. At Veracruz they could be loaded up with soldiers and arms. Several historians agree in calling it the first major amphibious landing in military history.

On March 9, 1847, General Scott led the amphibious landing of some 10,000 U.S. troops some three miles south of Veracruz itself in order to avoid the artillery fire from the city. *(Library of Congress)*

On March 9, 1847, as the Mexican Guardia still rampaged against its own government in Mexico City, Scott's forces set up at Sacrificios Island, some two and a half miles from Veracruz. Covered by a line of armed steamers, half a company of men each climbed into Scott's specially designed surf boats and began the landing on Veracruz's beachhead, outside the walls of the city. Veracruz was a salmon-colored, walled city ringed with nine forts. Overlooking the harbor was the huge, gloomy fortress, San Juan de Ulúa. The city was rumored to be the most heavily defended port in Mexico.

Indeed, though the news of the arrival of the U.S. Army came before them, the Mexicans stayed behind their walls and did nothing as the first 2,600 men leaped ashore. No doubt the citizens of Veracruz were disheartened by the failure of their own military to come to their rescue, but the U.S. troops were equally disappointed that they did not even get a chance to use a bayonet or a bowie knife. Only a few random shots of poor quality cannon issued from the city of Veracruz.

This contemporary lithograph depicts the devastating bombardment of the city of Veracruz by both the U.S. fleet offshore and artillery (some brought ashore from U.S. ships). *(Library of Congress)*

After several delays due to bad weather, on March 22, Scott turned his full force upon the city. With extra guns and gunners from the navy, Scott ordered massive shelling. One estimate was that 750 shells fell on Veracruz every 24 hours. After five days of this, the Veracruzianos surrendered. Mexican casualties numbered more than 1,100, many of them civilians killed not only by the American shells but by the collapsing buildings and such destruction; fewer than 100 Americans were killed or wounded.

Much of the city had been destroyed, and foreign consuls as well as ordinary Mexicans were outraged at his indiscriminate bombardment, especially as no one had had time to evacuate. Scott helped clear some of the rubble and, after reissuing his famous General Order No. 20, he severely punished any soldier who abused civilians or vandalized private property. He also took special care to see that church property was protected. But although the citizenry of a town occupied by Scott could expect to be safe from American soldiers, he seemed to have few regrets about the damage his siege visited upon the civilian population.

Back in the United States, however, many Americans, military as well as civilians, were shocked by the destruction. A critical view is

SCOTT'S DILEMMA
CREATING A PROFESSIONAL ARMY

Gen. Winfield Scott inherited a rowdy army from General Taylor, one which at times committed horrible acts against a fearful civilian population. To a man who always appeared in full dress uniform and paid strict attention to rank, this was appalling. His insistence on order off the battlefield as well as on it initiated a model of military discipline and professionalism.

On the other hand, a graver issue was at stake. Very simply, the United States itself was not geared up to be a war machine. The U.S. Military Academy at West Point (which was established in 1802) had not yet turned out many officers, and professional soldiery, with disciplined conduct and loyal commitment, was not yet a tradition. For example, on May 13, 1847, after successes at Veracruz and Buena Vista, the one-year term of service for 3,000 volunteers expired as a poorly conceived consequence of the War Bill passed in May 1846. Right in the middle of a war—and halfway to Mexico City—Scott was left with a mere 7,000 troops. Devoted to his men, Scott had nevertheless honored the release of the volunteers, with particular attention to seeing them off before the onset of the *vomito* (yellow fever) season at Veracruz.

Yet this did not stop Scott. Knowledgeable about military strategy and the science of war, he dared to take risks that belied his stuffy reputation. He was one of the first to recognize the value of light artillery. He dared, in the march through Jalapa and Puebla to Mexico City, to imitate Napoleonic strategy, and go beyond his supply lines so that he could advance quickly with optimum force. He did this despite his depleted numbers, for the death of the wounded had reduced Scott's remaining troops to under 6,000.

In Puebla, where he bivouacked (camped) for three months, Scott set about bringing order to civilian and military life. He organized local supply lines and developed a local intelligence network. It was not until July 1847 that reinforcements began to arrive—the 4,500 men who had set out from Veracruz beginning in early June. Scott, tactless and vain though he may have been, showed himself to be the country's first professional soldier.

offered through the diaries of U.S. Army colonel Ethan Hitchcock, who wrote a good deal about his misgivings about the war, as did others. He observed the violence of the U.S. siege of Veracruz:

On March 29, 1847, the fall of Veracruz was celebrated by the raising of the U.S. flag and by an artillery salute from the captured Castle of San Juan de Ulúa and U.S. ships. *(Library of Congress)*

I shall never forget the horrible fire of our mortars . . . going with dreadful certainty and bursting with sepulchral tones often in the center of private dwellings—it was awful. I shudder to think of it.

After the siege of Veracruz, one reporter observed, "all agree that the loss among the soldiery is comparatively small and the destruction among the women and children is very great." Just as in the 1960s, when many Americans became disillusioned with the Vietnam War, as news of the abuse and killing of innocent civilians trickled through, increasing numbers of Americans joined those already opposed to the war in Mexico.

"BIRDS OF PEACE AND BIRDS OF PREY"

On March 29, 1847, when Veracruz surrendered to the U.S. Army, the Mexicans were not the only people horrified by the destruction. So were many people in Europe and the United States. Nor was the strong reaction provoked by Scott's bombardment of Veracruz the first sign that many Americans were repulsed by the war in Mexico. Indeed, the antiwar movement that emerged during the Mexican War was in numerous ways the prototype for many that followed.

In the summer of 1846, Henry David Thoreau, a writer living in Concord, Massachusetts, refused to pay his taxes in protest against the war then under way in Mexico. He was put in jail. Another famous writer, Ralph Waldo Emerson, visited him and asked, "Henry, what are you doing in there?" Thoreau replied, "Ralph, what are you doing out there?"

Thoreau's friends paid the tax without his consent and he was released. He later wrote about his antiwar views in the famous essay known as "Civil Disobedience." In it, Thoreau laid out the principles of nonviolent noncooperation with what he considered an immoral act on the part of the government—waging the war. To this day, Thoreau's essay is one of the documents that pacifists and conscientious objectors refer back to when refusing to cooperate with military activities.

But it was not only intellectuals like Henry David Thoreau who were opposed to the war. Throughout the conflict, from the taking of Texas to the conquest of Mexico City, many U.S. citizens objected to the war with Mexico, some objecting on abstract moral or religious principles, some for more tangible practical or personal reasons. Lawmakers themselves were strongly divided. In 1844, for example,

Henry David Thoreau
(1817–62) (Library of
Congress)

President Tyler's first attempt to annex Texas was voted down in the
U.S. Senate, in part because some senators did not want to antagonize
Mexico but mostly because Texas would enter as a slaveholding state.

Even as Taylor became battle-ready along the banks of the Rio
Grande, the army itself was divided. Wrote U.S. Army colonel Ethan
Hitchcock, "We do not have a particle of right to be here . . . it looks
as if the government sent a small force on purpose to bring on a war,
as to [make up a reason] to take California." Hitchcock (and others)
continued to be skeptical as he observed the violence of the U.S. siege
of Veracruz. But, like many people, Hitchcock was not quite able to act
on his conscience: no, we should not be in Mexico, he clearly thought,
but he concluded, "My heart is not in this business . . . but, as a military
man, I am bound to execute orders."

For many reasons—some noble, some not so noble—even many
ordinary soldiers disliked the situation. Said one historian of the period:

Although they had volunteered to go to war . . . they did not
like the army, they did not like war, and generally speaking
they did not like Mexico or Mexicans.

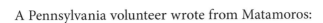

A Pennsylvania volunteer wrote from Matamoros:

> . . . tonight on drill an officer laid a soldier's skull open with his sword. But the time may come . . . when officers and men will stand on equal footing . . . A soldier's life is very disgusting.

As early as March of 1847, 9,207 men had deserted from the U.S. Army. It was a familiar story: Officers did well; recruits did poorly. The poor men took most of the casualties and most of the risks; they received little for their pains. Half of Taylor's army were recent immigrants, mostly Irish and German, who needed the money, and their patriotism was not high. And then there were stories of men being bribed to volunteer for the army with promises of money, land, and glory. The money did not necessarily appear. The land was not always there. As for glory, that soon faded in the light of miserable encampments and bloody battles.

For still other reasons, young men were not eager to join. As one anonymous young man wrote in the Cambridge, Massachusetts, *Chronicle:*

> I have no wish to participate in such "glorious" butcheries of women and children as were displayed in the capture of Monterrey, etc. Neither have I any desire to place myself under the dictation of a petty military tyrant . . . No Siree! As long as I can work, beg, or go to the poor house, I won't go to Mexico, to be lodged on the damp ground, half starved, half roasted, bitten by mosquitoes and centipedes, stung by scorpions and tarantulas— marched, drilled, and flogged, and then struck up to be shot at, for eight dollars a month and putrid rations.

Service in the army, in fact, was not very appealing at all. Food was of the poorest quality, clothes got completely soaked, and the hospitals were horribly overcrowded. Battle wounds were notoriously difficult to treat, and men died as much of infection as from whatever shells hit them. George B. McClellan, who later commanded the Army of the Potomac in the Civil War, complained that, "I have seen more suffering here than I could have imagined to exist. They [the troops] literally die like dogs."

VOLUNTEERS!

Men of the Granite State!

Men of Old Rockingham!! the strawberry-bed of patriotism, renowned for bravery and devotion to Country, rally at this call. Santa Anna, reeking with the generous confidence and magnanimity of your countrymen, is in arms, eager to plunge his traitor-dagger in their bosoms. To arms, then, and rush to the standard of the fearless and gallant CUSHING---put to the blush the dastardly meanness and rank toryism of Massachusetts. Let the half civilized Mexicans hear the crack of the unerring New Hampshire rifleman, and illustrate on the plains of San Luis Potosi, the fierce, determined, and undaunted bravery that has always characterized her sons.

Col. **THEODORE F. ROWE**, at No. 31 Daniel-street, is authorized and will enlist men this week for the Massachusetts Regiment of Volunteers. The compensation is **$10 per month---$30 in advance.** Congress will grant a handsome bounty in money and **ONE HUNDRED AND SIXTY ACRES OF LAND.**
Portsmouth, Feb. 2, 1847.

New Hampshire recruitment poster, 1847 (*Library of Congress*)

Officers complained that volunteers had no discipline and that it was impossible to get them to observe ordinary hygiene. Sometimes volunteers simply defied military discipline, and friction between officers and enlisted men continued throughout the war. As late as August 15, 1847, volunteers from Virginia, Mississippi, and North Carolina rebelled in northern Mexico against Col. Robert Treat Paine, one of Taylor's officers. During the mutiny, Paine killed one of his rebellious soldiers, and two of his lieutenants refused to help stop the rebellion. But all were forgiven in an attempt to maintain the unit's ability to fight.

On the home front, some of the more outspoken opposition to the war came from the churches, particularly the Congregationalists, Quakers, and Unitarians. In general, the churches and religious people who opposed the war in Mexico based their opposition on some of the same ideals that led them to oppose slavery in the United States.

Slavery itself, of course, was an inseparable part of the debate, for the most enthusiastic prowar people tended to be the proslavery Southerners. In the 1840s, the slave owners wanted to make sure that slavery was not abolished, and they were constantly looking for new slave states. President Polk's plan included accepting "Free-Soil" and slave states—Oregon and California as well as Texas. Conversely, people opposed to slavery thought the war was a big plot to keep that institution flourishing. In 1842, for example, that is what President Tyler's secretary of state, the famous Daniel Webster, thought about the campaign to acquire California. At the beginning of 1848, Frederick Douglass, a former slave, described the American desire for Mexican lands and its willingness to invade Mexico to get them as, "the present disgraceful, cruel, and iniquitous [unfair] war with our sister republic. Mexico seems a doomed victim to Anglo-Saxon cupidity [greed] and love of dominion."

Of course, when John O'Sullivan wrote his famous article on Manifest Destiny about the "will of Heaven" and how it was the United

This female figure, representing the United States leading pioneers and railroads westward, is an allegory of the concept of Manifest Destiny, which motivated many Americans to support the war with Mexico. *(Library of Congress)*

SLAVERY AND MANIFEST DESTINY

Mexico abolished slavery in 1829, just eight years after inviting Anglo settlers from North America into Texas. Despite agreeing to free their slaves, these settlers went back on their word repeatedly and were so resistant to abolition that, in 1830, Mexico prohibited further U.S. immigration into the territory. When Anglo-Texas won its freedom from Mexico, slavery was immediately secured by Texas's constitution.

While all eyes were on the Rio Grande in 1846, the slavery question rose again. Polk wanted congressional approval of $2 million to be appropriated for treaty negotiations with Mexico. However, David Wilmot, a Democratic representative from Pennsylvania, tacked the Wilmot Proviso onto it. The proviso stated that in no territory acquired "from the Republic of Mexico by the United States [would] . . . slavery nor involuntary servitude" be permitted. Polk was furious. He not only dreamt of the United States's seemingly God-given destiny to stretch "from sea to shining sea"—a doctrine at the core of Manifest Destiny—he was also proslavery. In fact, the Wilmot Proviso was blocked in the Senate and so was never passed.

Long after the U.S.-Mexican War ended, the *Charleston Mercury* (February 28, 1860) still mourned the loss of Southern opportunity:

We frequently talk of the future glories of our republican destiny on the continent, and of the spread of our civilization and free institutions over Mexico and the Tropics. Already we have absorbed two of her States, Texas and California. Is it expected that our onward march is to stop here? Is it not more probable and more philosophic to suppose that, as in the past, so in the future, the Anglo-Saxon race will, in the course of years, occupy and absorb the whole of that splendid but ill-peopled country, and to remove by gradual process, before them, the worthless mongrel races that now inhabit and curse the land? And in the accomplishment of this destiny is there a Southern man so bold as to say, the people of the South with their slave property are to consent to total exclusion?

No balder statement relating slavery and Manifest Destiny has been made.

States's right to take over all of Texas, then Oregon, then the whole continent, that simply egged on people who were eager to settle in the West. It made the Mexican War much more attractive. In turn, it made opponents to the war accuse its supporters of also being "land hungry." For nearly the whole time that the war was being fought, the debate raged on the floor of Congress as well. "In the matter of Mexicans upon their own soil," cried the powerful congressman from Ohio, Joshua Giddings, "or in robbing them of their country, I can take no part in either, now or hereafter! . . . The guilt of these crimes must rest on others—I will not participate in them!" Senator H. V. Johnson retorted that though "War has its evils" it was also, in his mind, the instrument of "human elevation and human happiness."

"We must march," said one Congressman Giles from Maryland, "from Texas straight to the Pacific Ocean, and be bound only by its roaring wave. It is the destiny of the white race, it is the destiny of the Anglo-Saxon race . . ." Not so, replied the American Anti-Slavery Society some days later. The war, in their opinion, was "waged solely for the detestable and horrible purpose of extending slavery throughout the vast territory of Mexico."

But when push came to shove, all but the strongly antislavery Whigs had voted with the majority for war. Why? For one, hunger for more land was real. The opposition party, the Whigs, may have been against the war but land tempted them. More land meant more opportunities for business. Secondly, most lawmakers did not want to be accused of putting U.S. soldiers in danger by not paying for enough supplies. When President Polk's original war message claimed that "American blood was spilled on American soil," a young representative from Illinois, Abraham Lincoln, challenged President Polk to point out the exact spot. Yet once hostilities broke out, Lincoln would not vote against supplying the troops.

While Scott was en route to Tampico on the first stage of his campaign to take Mexico City, back in December 7, 1846, the 29th Congress reconvened for its second session. The war was still being hotly debated. When President Polk gave his second annual address to Congress on December 8, he made his own feelings quite clear: Voicing opposition to the war was giving "aid and comfort" to the Mexican opponents. Despite Polk's attempt to pressure Congress into sup-

"SHOW ME THE SPOT!"
LINCOLN OPPOSES THE WAR

One member of the House of Representatives was especially skeptical in his objections to the war. In a speech made on the House floor on December 22, 1847, young Abraham Lincoln, a representative from Illinois, challenged President Polk. In detail, Lincoln questioned Polk's justification for military action—that blood "of our citizens" had been shed on "our own soil." Painstakingly Lincoln asked for seven proofs. He asked the precise location of the spot: "Was [it] or was [it] not, within the territories of Spain" that had become, through the Mexican Revolution, Mexico and within a settlement of people in the area long before Texas came about? Were people in this settlement consensual or involuntary taxpayers, participants in Texan or U.S. government there? Did these people flee the U.S. Army's approach *before* blood was shed? Were "our citizens" actually soldiers, sent into "that settlement by the military order of the President. . . ?"

Lincoln clearly was suggesting that the United States had invaded Mexico. But Polk had got what he wanted, while Lincoln's stand made him so unpopular in his home district that he did not even bother to seek reelection.

A young Abraham Lincoln objected to President Polk's handling of the conflict in Mexico. *(Library of Congress)*

porting "his" war, legislators still debated—as they would do in later decades—the right to declare and wage war.

Further, the war effort needed money, and in that same address, Polk reintroduced the Two Million Bill—only now it had been increased to a $3 Million Bill. "I wonder," thundered Garrett Davis of Kentucky, "by what imperial or regal authority his majesty [Polk] undertook to act [to initiate this war]." Even some slave owners disapproved of Polk:

Meredith P. Gentry called Polk a "petty usurper" and Robert Toombs charged that Polk had illegally seized the power to make war by invading Mexico and seizing Mexican territory.

Yet, fearful of being accused of not giving U.S. soldiers adequate supplies and sufficient arms, the same antiwar Congress approved the $3 million bill to pay for the war on February 17, 1847. Furthermore, Congress did not accept the reintroduced Wilmot Proviso, which forbade slavery in any territory acquired from Mexico.

But even as Polk and his cabinet urged Scott on to Veracruz and Mexico City, the U.S. Whigs continued to protest the war. They charged that the war was bankrupting the country, that it was unjust and inhumane. On the very day that Scott's armada set sail from Isla Lobos toward Veracruz—March 2, 1847—antislavery and antiwar senator Thomas L. Corwin of Ohio made his most famous condemnation of the war:

> If I were a Mexican I would tell you, "Have you not room in your own country to bury your dead men? If you come into mine, we will greet you with bloody hands, and welcome you to hospitable graves."

In short, the war was neither popular nor easy to wage. Even when the news of Taylor's victory at Buena Vista reached Washington on April 1, 1847, the brief surge of pride in the U.S. fighting force that Polk hoped would boost support for his side failed to materialize. With such victories as Buena Vista, the antiwar forces argued, Mexico had been sufficiently punished, Tampico was protected, so why not get the United States out of this ridiculous war?

From start to finish, then, many civilians, civil servants, and military men had serious objections to the wisdom of carrying on this war. Aside from the moral objections and the expense, there was also the sheer bungling that plagued the war effort—problems of command, incredibly inefficient communications, and such fiascos as trying to bribe Santa Anna or undermine Mexico's opposition from within. To many Americans, especially those concentrated along the eastern seaboard, the war with Mexico seemed very remote and impractical.

And what of the ordinary people who were most affected by this war, the North Americans residing in the Southwest? Although many descriptions of the early Southwest focus on such characters,

(continues on page 102)

A JUST WAR?

Thinkers on international law since St. Augustine (354–430) and St. Thomas Aquinas (1225–74) have developed seven principles or considerations to determine whether a war is "just" or legitimate. Those in favor and those against the U.S.-Mexican War have tended, either explicitly or indirectly, to debate the war in terms of these principles.

1. A just war must be authorized by a legitimate authority.

    Proponents: At news of the hostilities at Matamoros, President Polk asked Congress to vote for war, and after a bitter debate the House voted 174 to 14 and the Senate 40 to 2 to support the president.

    Opponents: Various congressmen expressed concern that the United States was rushing into a war with less than complete knowledge of the situation, while antislavery representatives, especially from New England, argued that it was essentially a "land grab" to add more slave states to the Union.

2. A just war can only be fought if it is started with right intentions, such as to redress a wrong.

    Proponents: Territory between the Nueces River and the Rio Grande was U.S. territory, and Gen. Taylor's orders to blockade an international boundary at the mouth of the Rio Grande on April 12, 1845, were justified by the movement of Mexican troops into that territory. Thus, the attack on U.S. troops at the Carrecitos ranch took place on American soil.

    Opponents: Texas had been Mexican territory and then a republic wrested from Mexico by largely slaveholding settlers who had defied Mexico's prohibition against slavery. As the southernmost Texas settlement was short of the Nueces River at Corpus Christi, the Rio Grande was well within Mexican Territory, and the U.S. Army had invaded Mexico.

3. A war cannot be justified if its chances of success are low and it appears that it will drag on for an extended period.

    Proponents: Although the U.S. Army at the outset of the war was not especially large or well trained or equipped, the United States clearly had the means to upgrade its forces, while the Mexican army was less likely to be able to match the U.S. improvements.

Opponents: General Santa Anna was a professional soldier, well schooled in Napoléonic army strategies, and his troops were professional solders. They were also fighting on home ground.

4. The damage of the war must be proportional to the injury suffered.

Proponents: Although the casualties of the U.S. Army would be some 15,000 men, the territory gained—approximately 500,000 square miles of land, from Texas to California, and the present-day U.S. Southwest—justified this risk.

Opponents: The casualties inflicted on both the U.S. and Mexican forces were far out of proportion to the disputes that were used as the basis for engaging in warfare.

5. A just war should be waged only as a last resort.

Proponents: President Polk had sent John Slidell to Mexico to negotiate a settlement over the nations' disputes, but the Mexican government refused to deal with him. Meanwhile, Polk had made it clear that he would take action at the first sign of just one hostile act on Mexico's part, and he regarded the Mexicans' conduct at Matamoros as an attack on U.S. soil.

Opponents: The U.S. terms that Polk and Slidell were prepared to offer Mexico were obviously unacceptable to the Mexican people. The territory along the Nueces River was in dispute, and more time and effort should have been devoted to resolving this issue, as so many other international boundary disputes were settled.

6. The real reason for the war should show right intent and should be the stated reason.

Proponents: The United States had been patient, but events at Matamoras were the last straw. The United States could not allow its armed forces to be attacked. Besides, Mexico was indebted to the United States for damages to U.S. citizens and property in its frequent and bloody revolutions.

Opponents: The Mexican debt should not be an excuse to make war any more than the much larger U.S. international debt would be. And rather than Matamoros being the "last straw," as Polk claimed, the United States entered the war basically to acquire more territory in pursuit of its "manifest destiny."

(continues)

(continued)

7. The goal of a just war should be to reestablish peace. The peace established after the war should be better than the peace that would exist if the war were not fought.

Proponents: Peace and prosperity were in fact established across a vast territory that had at best languished under Mexican rule. Mexico was free to pursue its own destiny, and the two nations would never again resort to war.

Opponents: The so-called peace imposed on Mexico left it with a humiliating defeat, took away a large and valuable territory, and sowed many of the seeds for ongoing difficult relations between the United States and Mexico. As for the United States, the new territory acquired only aggravated the issue over slavery, and not long afterward the United States was embroiled in its own civil war.

(continued from page 99)

the ordinary person in Mexican territory was neither a gun-slinging Anglo or a knife-throwing Spaniard. Violence among civilians was an exception. Shoot-outs and other kinds of violence were stories for the next century's movies rather than real life, and even along the border, chance meetings were usually peaceful. What was important to Anglo-Americans and Mexicans alike was making a living. They were trappers and hunters, farmers, cattle ranchers, and merchants who needed one another to survive. They needed imported goods as well. Muskets, rifles, salt, and coffee came from faraway places. The California cattle-raising industry needed the help of eastern marketing and shipping. In New Mexico, Santa Fe was a cosmopolitan center where purveyors of goods and services met and exchanged currencies on a regular basis, without much attention to where the trader came from. Mexicans traded pack animals and their fine horses, their silver and gold, for Anglo weapons and cloth.

For the average *estadosunidenses* settlers, the move out west was made for economic reasons. In the 1830s, U.S. land cost $1.25 an acre—expensive then—while in Tampico, for example, it cost only 12.5 cents an acre. People could not buy land on credit in the United States. Obviously, cheap land appealed to people who wanted to improve their lives.

When Anglo-Americans and Mexicans became neighbors they did not necessarily stand apart. Some married each other; some Anglos, converted to Catholicism. They even grew to like one another. Said one *estadounidenseano* when he visited California in the 1830s: "A common bullock driver delivering a message, seemed to speak like an ambassador at an audience."

And the Mexicans admired the new settlers' way of doing business. Recorded in the proceedings of the San Antonio town council was the following:

> The industrious, honest North American settlers have raised cotton and cane, and erected gins and saw mills. Their industry has made them comfortable and independent while the Mexican settlements, depending on the pay of soldiers among them for money, have lagged far behind.

This statement led up to an appeal to allow more North American settlers to help develop the area.

On the other hand, admiration for Yanqui (Yankee) ingenuity was more common among the upper-class Mexicans, and even there some anti-U.S. sentiment also existed. The *ricos,* the wealthy Mexicans, were very cultivated and thought the U.S. frontiersmen crude. The European literature that many well-educated Mexicans read looked down on the Anglo-Saxons and blamed them for the greed and misfortunes of the Industrial Revolution. In turn, early American writings had their share of nasty remarks about their Spanish-speaking neighbors. Many Protestants despised Catholicism and did not mind saying so. Many Anglos were shamelessly racist, despising their neighbors for the color of their skin and the notion that they were not racially "pure." Still other North Americans looked down on the social system of their neighbors, not without some accuracy. "The entire business of the country is in the hands of the rich . . . and as a natural consequence the rich know no end to their treasure, nor the poor to their poverty," wrote one U.S. pioneer from California.

The ordinary U.S. settler was accustomed to doing things his way and did not want to give up what privileges he had in the States. Mexicans thought the newcomers should follow their laws just like everyone else, and they were angered that so many settlers from the United States would not honor the Mexican prohibition against slavery.

Quite aside from all such reasons, though, the majority of Mexicans had been astonished at the U.S. invasion of their territory. For one thing, the Mexicans thought the dispute with Britain over Oregon would distract Polk and the American government more than it did; the Mexicans assumed that England would do nothing that made it easy for Texas to join the U.S. Further, the Mexicans thought there could be little threat from the U.S. armed forces. Mexican soldiers outnumbered U.S. soldiers five to one, and the Mexican officers, at least, were regarded as being highly professional—not (they thought) like so many *estadosunidenses,* money-grubbing creatures too soft to fight. Many Europeans viewed U.S. chances of victory in this same way. The *Times* (London) scoffed, "Invasion and conquest of a vast region by a State [nation] which is without an army and without credit is a novelty among nations."

But if the Mexicans or the world at large still had any doubts about the efficacy of U.S. armed forces by March 1847, they were all about to be disabused as General Scott prepared for the assault on Mexico City.

TO THE HALLS OF MONTEZUMA

Despite the civilian outcry about the violent taking of Veracruz, Scott had no choice but to press on with his campaign. He immediately refocused his aim on the ultimate goal: taking Mexico City, thereby cutting off Mexico's head so that its body would be powerless. But between the taking of Veracruz in March 1847 and the taking of Mexico City in September 1847 lay a tale of epic—and occasionally comic—proportions.

Mexicans as well as Americans would be involved in the convoluted struggles that accompanied this march to the capital. Shortly after Santa Anna put down the Polkos Rebellion, in March, Scott reported to Secretary of War Marcy that Santa Anna was now "in full possession of the executive authority . . . There is no longer an opposing party in arms." That is, the Mexicans were not united against the United States.

At the same time, Scott and his troops were desperately trying to get out of the fever zone, the *tierra caliente* ("hot land"), where shortly began the season for *vomito,* or yellow fever. The immediate goal was to get his forces up to *tierra templada,* or the areas of temperate climate— Jalapa, Puebla, the towns of the highlands on the road to Mexico City. His optimism ran high. While, Scott reported to Marcy, he would continue to advance, he had spoken carefully to several high-ranking prisoners from Veracruz. To Scott, it seemed that there was a willingness to discuss peace. What Scott overlooked was the fact that though the Mexican congress had given enormous power to Santa Anna, it did not give him the power to make peace.

Jalapa, in the highlands, was Scott's immediate destination for his troops. Dividing his army into two divisions, Worth's and Twiggs's, Scott sent Twiggs's out first, on April 8, but without sufficient horses and wagons. Dragging the machinery of war and the necessary food, water, and medicines up into the highlands was a huge task. Twiggs's sole guide was a book of memoirs by Frances (Fanny) Calderón de la Barca—both Scott and Marcy had recommended it and read it themselves—as well as an 1843 classic, Prescott's *History of the Conquest of Mexico.*

Frances Calderón, Scottish wife of the first ambassador from the king of Spain to the Republic of Mexico, at least gave a reasonably accurate description of the territory. Veracruz was muggy, hot, feverish; the adjacent lands would be sandy. The first day out of the city, Twiggs pushed his army as fast as he could through the expected terrain—nothing but sand hills, sand flats, sand valleys, sand, sand, sand, and spiky-leaved palmetto bushes. But he lost too many men to exhaustion, and too many goods were cast off to lighten the load. Twiggs slowed the pace, and they soon passed out of the sandy area into a greener, lush one. All of this belonged to Santa Anna—the paved road they walked on, several huge and beautiful homes along the way, stone arched bridges. Twiggs stopped to rest at the village of Río del Plan, for a steep, terrible ascent into the highlands that now lay ahead of them.

On April 5, Santa Anna had arrived in Jalapa after marching his weary troops from Mexico City. But the Mexican troops were hardly

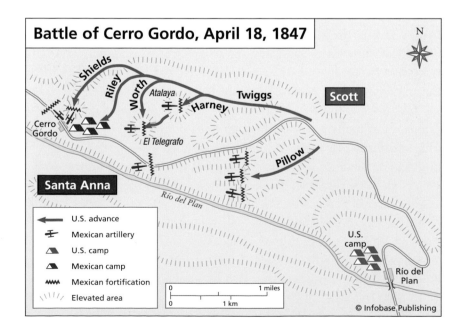

Battle of Cerro Gordo, April 18, 1847

DID LEE AND GRANT MEET DURING THE WAR IN MEXICO?

In popular histories of the Civil War, it is often stated that when Gen. Robert E. Lee surrendered to Gen. Ulysses S. Grant at Appomattox Court House, they were meeting for at least the second time in their careers. This would not seem wholly unreasonable—both were West Point graduates who had served many years in the army. And it certainly would make a fine moral lesson for a nation seeking to come together: two old army "buddies" who had fought hard but were now "making up." But to begin with, Lee and Grant were almost different generations. Lee had graduated from West Point in 1829, Grant in 1843, and an examination of their military careers reveals that they had never been assigned to the same posts or regions until the war in Mexico. The occasion cited for their meeting in Mexico—if one is even cited—is a day when Lee, as an aide to Gen. Winfield Scott, made an inspection visit to the unit where Grant was quartermaster. In his memoirs, however, Grant makes no reference to such an occasion. How then did the legend grow up? In his memoirs, Grant does once say, "I knew Lee personally," but the context suggests that he is referring to Lee's character and his manner of command. Then in his account of their meeting at Appomattox Court House, Grant writes: "[Lee] remarked that he remembered me very well in the old army; and I told him that as a matter of course I remembered him perfectly, but from the difference in our rank and years . . . I had thought it very likely that I had not attracted his attention sufficiently to be remembered by him after such a long interval." It seems clear that Grant is diplomatically saying that he suspects Lee was simply being polite in claiming he knew him. In any case, neither Grant nor Lee ever explicitly referred to having met in person before the surrender.

amateurs. With a quick rest, the Mexicans were ordered to march east toward Río del Plan and a big hill, Cerro Gordo, opposing it. There they took positions against the Twiggs forces climbing that way. What Santa Anna hoped to do was to keep the U.S. forces from advancing above the yellow fever level—what guns would not do, the mosquito would.

On April 11, having heard about the Mexican army threatening Twiggs, Scott left hastily for Jalapa. At noon, on April 14, he was at Río del Plan. The Mexicans were across the river, at Cerro Gordo. Although their numbers were about equal—roughly 8,000 to 9,000 each—in that position, the Mexicans would be looking down their gun barrels at the U.S. troops.

And that meant that the Americans had to sneak around to the back door. Ordered to do some reconnaissance, a 40-year-old captain with bright blue eyes led a group through dense vegetation, up the spine of a fingerlike hill and behind the left flank of Santa Anna's army. Realizing the importance of the route, Capt. Robert E. Lee sent for guns and ammunition. Slowly and ever so silently, the men tied up their artillery ("24-pounders") with rope and raised them through the trees. At times, according to another young officer, Lt. Ulysses S. Grant, the men had to lower them back down again to follow their gunners up and down the treacherous chasms. All this while they were surrounded by the sound of guns echoing through the hills where other battles were raging.

Up the perilous slope, as though they were carrying, not weapons of war, but so many eggs, moved Lee's troops. Suddenly, they burst

Colonel William S. Harney was a veteran cavalry officer from Tennessee and gained fame when on April 17, 1847, he led a bold charge up to the height of Cerro Gordo and engaged the Mexicans in direct combat. *(Library of Congress)*

In one of the more embarrassing moments in Mexican military history, General Santa Anna and his staff fled from Cerro Gordo on the morning of the second day of the battle after realizing that the U.S. forces were about to triumph. *(Library of Congress)*

out onto the top of a hill, bowie knives bared, guns blazing. Only a few Mexican soldiers occupied the top and they scattered in seconds. At the height of the battle, these courageous Americans had climbed up and seized the Mexicans' own guns and turned the guns on them. Another unit cut off the Mexicans' escape route along the highway. The entire left flank of Santa Anna's force broke formation and fled into the hills and the fever zone, the river valley. American losses were some 63 killed and 350 wounded; Mexican losses were never officially reported, but their dead and wounded were probably about 1,000, with roughly 3,000 taken prisoner.

On April 18, victorious U.S. troops en route to Jalapa broke into an estate. It was yet another one of Santa Anna's magnificent houses, filled with ornate paintings, fine statues, and fountains. There they came away with a unique souvenir. It was Santa Anna's spare wooden leg, which has remained on display in Springfield, Illinois, since the 1920s. On April 19, the U.S. Army rode into Jalapa after a minor skirmish at its guardian fortress of Perote. By now, the Mexicans must have thought that the invading American soldiers were invincible.

Yet the Mexican soldiers had the central valley leading to Mexico City well fortified. Scott did not even consider taking that route but, instead, instructed Worth and his division to take Puebla, halfway between Veracruz and the capital. Scott fired off a decree urging the inhabitants not to seek allies across the Atlantic; reminding them delicately of their poor military performance, he wrote, "Remember that you are Americans and that your happiness is not to come from Europe."

With barely a night of rest, Worth's division marched toward Puebla, the second-largest city in Mexico at that time. The townspeople were not Santa Anna supporters. Rather, they supported the conservative Mexican Catholic Church and probably some of them even wanted monarchy. Santa Anna, for obvious reasons, decided not to challenge the U.S. troops there.

At Jalapa, Scott had to let 3,000 of his men go home, for their term of service had expired. No one had told them it was going to be like this—the disease, the hard marches, making camp in the heat of the jungle one night and sleeping in the freezing mountain air the next, the disfigurement and death. Sometimes they had not gotten paid; sometimes they went hungry. So they returned to the United States.

Of those who remained, many were ill. Although they had climbed out of the *tierra caliente* (the fever zone) at Jalapa and into what many compared to the Garden of Eden, some of Twiggs's men had not climbed fast enough. A number of the men in Worth's division were ill, too. Instead of North American supermen, as the inhabitants of Puebla had expected, a long line of dusty, ragged, and bone-weary men trudged into their city, some whose guns were no less battered than their bodies.

The U.S. forces remained in Puebla for more than three months, their numbers dipping below 10,000. Four hundred wagons and 1,200 mules piled with supplies tried to make it through from Veracruz, but the caravans were assaulted by guerrillas in the hills. Soldiers who stayed there died by the hundreds from the fever. The Poblanos, as the people of Puebla were called, were proper "hosts," though not all that friendly. It was as though the whole war had stalled. Both sides fell back exhausted by their battles and by the politics and intrigues of their superiors.

All this while, Polk was also trying to open up negotiations for peace through the State Department. He chose not to send Secretary of State James Buchanan to negotiate in Mexico—he would not have been aggressive enough, Polk felt—and, for fear of being accused of patron-age, he passed over his friend Senator Benton. In order to pave the way for peace talks, he and his cabinet selected the less threatening Nicholas P. Trist, a high-ranking member of the State Department, former con-sul at Havana, Cuba, a West Point graduate, fluent in Spanish—what more could Polk and his government ask for? The cabinet unanimously endorsed Polk's candidate as a peace negotiator.

Trist left on April 16, the day after the cabinet confirmed his posi-tion. Polk wanted to keep the mission a secret because he thought the Whigs would try to block Trist's efforts—although the entire story behind his journey was published four days later in the *New York Her-ald*. What Trist was to offer was really very simple: The U.S.-Mexican border should be at about where it is today, and Mexico should give the United States the vast Mexican provinces of New Mexico and California in exchange for $15 million. Trist was also permitted to offer between $20 million and $30 million if he found he was able to squeeze more territory from Santa Anna's government.

Even then the president was of two minds. One mind wanted a treaty and the other wanted a stunning military victory. In fact, at the same time that he and his cabinet were working out the terms they wished Trist to negotiate, Polk wrote to another "mustang general," (appointed through political favoritism rather than a military person risen in the ranks), Gideon Pillow, "If they still refuse to negotiate for peace, you may rely upon my fixed purpose to prosecute the war, with the utmost possible vigour." Pillow's assignment to Mexico, however, was an example of Polk's favoritism overcoming good judgment. Pillow was with Scott during the Veracruz to Puebla campaign and, knowing nothing of military matters in the first place, he proved himself to be a timid and fumbling officer. He was better known among the soldiers as "Polk's Spy."

Trist was a far more serious and substantial individual, although Scott snidely referred to Trist as a lowly clerk who was pompous and self-important about his mission to Mexico. Some historians repeated that insult as fact. Actually Trist was second in command among professionals at the State Department. The fact is, too, that Nicholas P. Trist must have had a bit of the adventurer in him, as much as the would-be statesman. The journey, in those days, between Washington and New Orleans, the major port city from which all ships bound for Mexico seemed to leave, took days of horse-drawn discomfort. Once in

New Orleans, Trist adopted a pseudonym—"Doctor Tarreau"—so that no one would know that a U.S. official was on his way to Mexico. Then, in the hustle of ships whose holds carried everything from cotton bales to molasses to human beings in chains, Trist found a revenue cutter (an armed government vessel), the *Ewing*. It was this ship that carried him to Veracruz. During the eight days at sea, the former "Doctor Tarreau's" illusions grew as he saw himself bringing peace to the toiling soldiers in Mexico.

The *Ewing* slid into the harbor at Veracruz on May 6, 1847, just as the heat and the fever season were beginning to make human life miserable. The U.S. officials who met Trist there were polite, but not terribly interested in listening to Trist try to order them about. He demanded a detachment of men on horseback, and gave them a letter he had written to Scott rather than show Scott two official documents from William Marcy, the secretary of war, and from James Buchanan, secretary of state. Both would have explained Trist's mission better and with more tact.

After a difficult night's sleep, Trist prepared to catch up to Scott at Jalapa. That meant the uncomfortable, dangerous journey through the fever zone and through territory now filled with bandits. When a detachment of 40 cavalrymen trotted up the steep streets of Jalapa on May 7, they brought Trist's letter to Scott. Upon opening it, so the story goes, the general flew into a rage. He read out loud such phrases as "clothed with such diplomatic powers as will authorize him to enter into arrangements with the government of Mexico for suspension of hostilities"—what was this nonsense? Scott took up his pen and dashed off his brief reply to Trist. He sent a copy to Secretary of War Marcy, which included the accusation that the "Secretary of War proposes to degrade me, by requiring that I, the commander of this army, shall defer to you, the chief clerk of the Department of State, the question of continuing or discontinuing" the war.

Back and forth went the notes. First Trist decided to go home. Then Trist asked the English representative in Mexico City to help contact the Mexicans. When the representative, Sir Edward Thornton, arrived at headquarters in Puebla—where both Scott and Trist had moved to by that time—he had struggled over difficult terrain only to find that Scott and Trist were not even speaking to each other. And Polk was angry at Scott because Scott seemed to think only he could communicate with the Mexican government. Both Scott and Trist were in danger of being fired.

The Mexican government, meanwhile, was in its usual state of uproar. Santa Anna had lost Cerro Gordo, though how was a matter that made everyone shake their heads in disbelief. The Mexican congress, now doubting whether Santa Anna was even to be trusted, in April passed a law that anyone negotiating privately with the United States would be considered a traitor. But such a law obviously conflicted with the powers of the Mexican president to negotiate for peace, and secret communications left the Mexican capital with hints that perhaps peace might be negotiated.

Just when the British emissary Thornton found Scott and Trist ignoring each other in Puebla, Polk succeeded in getting Congress to pass the bill that would appropriate the $3 million that would, among other goals, help secure a treaty. This was immediately condemned by Mexican government leaders as an attempt at bribery by the Americans. The Mexicans wanted peace but . . . Some of them asked Trist what was the meaning of this $3 Million Bill? Trist pleaded innocent; no, he responded, not for bribery. But, Trist admitted, Polk had given him permission to offer a generous sum if Mexico would agree to the Rio Grande as the boundary between itself and the United States.

So the negotiations went slowly. Then Santa Anna let it be known that he might be interested in some cash for himself and his friends—just $10,000 to be divided up among Santa Anna's "associates." Then just $1 million when peace was concluded. Nothing so extravagant as $3 million. Trist was so shocked by this development that he immediately went to Scott to bury the hatchet. He promptly fell ill; Scott sent him a jar of marmalade, and by the time he recovered he and Scott had become fast friends. They vowed that Santa Anna was not going to pull the wool over their eyes. But the intrigue continued, and even General Pillow got into the act as $10,000 mysteriously slipped into Santa Anna's pockets.

When Santa Anna went back to his congress to get support for his efforts at settling with the United States, his political opponents got back at him by not showing up in enough numbers to provide the legal quorum. Santa Anna decided that since he was president, he would proceed to negotiate himself. Just in case, however, Santa Anna asked Scott to start marching toward the capital. The threat of the enemy attacking the capital should provide the Mexican congress with the proper incentive. Already, Gen. Gabriel Valencia was standing by with a force of 4,000, ready to defend the city.

Santa Anna now told a friend, Salvador Bermúdez de Castro, the Spanish ambassador to Mexico, that he would become dictator as soon as the *estadounidenses* attacked the defenders of the city. Then he would make peace with them. But, California, he assured his countrymen—we will never give up California! With peace waiting in the wings, the stage was set for still another battle.

Some historians have suggested that when Santa Anna accepted the bribe he was really buying time for the Mexican army to prepare for the next attack. Certainly Santa Anna recruited more soldiers and fortified the road to Mexico City while Scott and his army, garrisoned at Puebla, grew soft. But, in Mexico City, when the word leaked out that Santa Anna was trying his hand at negotiating with the enemy, there were cries of treason. Some wanted to see him hanging from the gallows, while others wondered if *el Presidente* had gone mad. By now, though, some 25,000 to 30,000 Mexican soldiers were in and around Mexico City, just waiting for Scott's army.

Meanwhile, the U.S. forces were beginning to put into place a noose around the Mexican capital. General Wool's troops were in a small circle up in the northwest from Chihuahua to Baja California; General Taylor blocked off the northeast from his position near Saltillo at Buena Vista; to the southeast were Scott and his armies. By August, the U.S. forces had grown to about 14,000, despite the sickness and the loss of men who wanted to go home. But Mexican guerrillas filled the highlands, and Scott could not get anything more than messages through the lawless territory between Puebla and Veracruz.

Scott, as demonstrated at Veracruz, could be relentless when he felt the need. So long as supplies piled up at the docks of Veracruz, Scott tried anything he could think of to get at them. No matter what Santa Anna was plotting, the North American general had a war to fight. Despite previous scruples, Scott got the Texas Rangers to serve as couriers and even paid Mexican bandits to work as assassins against the guerrillas.

Further, though the Guardia Nacional had just concluded the Polkos Rebellion, they would have mutinied once more had they known that Santa Anna, the hero of the glorious revolution, was secretly bargaining with the *gringos* and had sent a sealed dispatch to General Scott. His offer was simple: If he allowed Scott and his

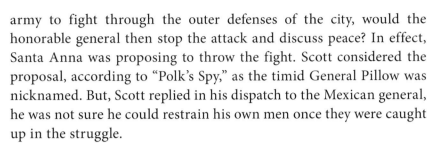

army to fight through the outer defenses of the city, would the honorable general then stop the attack and discuss peace? In effect, Santa Anna was proposing to throw the fight. Scott considered the proposal, according to "Polk's Spy," as the timid General Pillow was nicknamed. But, Scott replied in his dispatch to the Mexican general, he was not sure he could restrain his own men once they were caught up in the struggle.

All summer, U.S. troops assumed that Scott intended to attack Mexico City. From the north, Taylor sent as many men as he could spare to join the fray. The few remaining spread out along the boundaries or went to reinforce Veracruz and catch one more round of yellow fever. One officer, future president Franklin Pierce, ordered to bring reinforcements to Scott, managed his transport very efficiently: He lost one soldier to the fever at Veracruz, and none on the march. Although he was delayed because two bridges blew up and he was attacked five times, on August 6, he arrived at Puebla, unharmed and unruffled. Pierce's troops were the last of the U.S. reinforcements. Then, with 10,738 men—and though 2,000 were sick with the fever—Scott set out for the capital. Writing to Secretary of War Marcy, he compared himself to Cortez, the Spanish conqueror, determined to be a "self-sustaining [fighting] machine."

Ahead of his fighting force, Scott had sent his engineers. Back and forth they trotted with their instruments, measuring and sighting and taking notes. They managed to get all the way to the northern rim of the mountains surrounding the valley where Mexico City was located, and returned with a remarkably accurate map for their general. It showed Mexico City rising almost like a fortress west of marshes that had once been artificial lakes—Chalco, Xochimilco, the large Texcoco—built by the Aztecs. Long stone causeways stretched over these marshes toward the capital; just getting onto these causeways would be a challenge to Scott and his troops because the approaches were narrow and treacherous. Rather than meet the enemy head on, Scott decided to outflank the Mexican army by approaching from the south and southwest.

It was as if the ghosts of the first brutal battles for Mexico hovered over the valley. The *norteamericanos* trudged toward it, ragged and worn-looking, flesh sizzling under the unkind rays of the mid-August sun. Santa Anna waited just as Montezuma had some 327 years previously, as if that same Mexican sun could magically save him.

This is a view of Mexico City as seen from the Convent of San Cosme. Located on the edge of the city, U.S. troops would pass by it when they entered the Mexican capital. *(Library of Congress)*

Santa Anna dragged his artillery (which included 90 guns) ahead of 20,000 troops and drew up their line of battle along the eastern road to the city. When Scott's forces took their positions on the southern approaches, Santa Anna moved some of his men westward to prevent the U.S. troops from turning around. A group under General Pillow gathered around the Pedregal, a lava formation like a petrified sea southwest of Mexico City. Along one side ran the original road that Cortez took into the old Aztec capital. Pillow was neither as clever nor as vicious as Cortez; he attacked too early and the Mexicans, under General Valencia, beat his troops back in no time.

Then, while the Mexican troops celebrated their victory over Pillow, Scott sneaked over the Pedregal lava at night and, on August 20, the Americans surprised Valencia and defeated him at Contreras, just south of the Pedregal. Santa Anna evaded Scott, however, for he did not come to Valencia's rescue. However, Scott circled around to the north and engaged Santa Anna at a fortresslike convent called Churubusco, where he and Worth defeated the general. It was a particularly brutal fight, according to one witness:

Those fields around Churubusco were now covered with thousands of human casualties and with mangled bodies of horses and mules that blocked roads and filled ditches. Four thousand Mexicans lay dead or wounded . . .

Not only were so many Mexicans killed, but 1,000 Americans—one out of seven—were killed, wounded, or counted as missing.

More recently, some war historians have suggested that at Churubusco Scott almost lost the war. It cost him 1,000 of his best men just to take this convent. Much of the heavy fire was delivered by the San Patricio Brigade, the Irish unit that had taken up arms with the Mexicans nearly two years before. Many San Patricios died defending the convent at Churubusco, long after running out of ammunition, and 69 were captured. They had to be placed under guard to keep their former companions-in-arms from harming them; but when the city finally fell, U.S. troops branded the San Patricios' cheeks with a *D* (for "deserter") and hanged them.

Scott then proceeded farther northwest to the next little settlement, Tacubaya. There, it could be said, he had broken through the defenses to Mexico City and not yet entered it. Now Santa Anna asked for a truce. Begging the North Americans not to sack the city, the Mexican foreign minister, Gen. Ramón Pacheco, asked the British to help work

This lithograph depicts the Battle of Churubusco on August 20, 1847. Located three miles from Mexico City, Churubusco was a convent that the Mexicans turned into a fortress, but after a deadly battle it fell to U.S. troops. *(Library of Congress)*

out an agreement. There was an exchange of remarks between Santa Anna and Scott and an all-night brainstorming session between U.S. and Mexican commissioners, but the Armistice of Tacubaya went into effect on August 24, 1847.

Before Santa Anna signed the armistice, he called for a meeting of Mexico's congress to speak to them about signing a peace treaty with the invaders. The congressmen refused to attend, but the stubborn Santa Anna assigned José Joaquín Herrera, Bernardo Couto, and Ignacio Mora y Vallamil as commissioners to work on a settlement. The armistice, and perhaps the forming of a commission itself, was a temporary solution that was meant to last only until more substantial agreements could be worked out. It lasted all of 16 days. From August 27 to September 6, 1847, these statesmen met with Trist in a valiant effort to work something out.

Representatives of the two nations argued about the boundary between Mexico and Texas. They argued about slavery—to be prohibited from any territory acquired from Mexico. They quibbled about

On September 8, 1847, U.S. forces attacked one of the final fortresses defending Mexico City, the Molina del Rey ("mill of the king"). After suffering many casualties, U.S. forces prevailed. *(Library of Congress)*

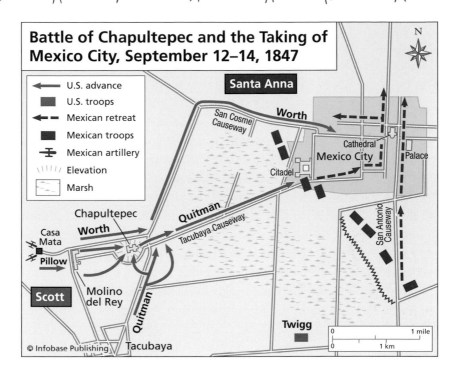

Battle of Chapultepec and the Taking of Mexico City, September 12–14, 1847

N

- ← U.S. advance
- ■ U.S. troops
- ←-- Mexican retreat
- ■ Mexican troops
- ⊥ Mexican artillery
- \||// Elevation
- Marsh

Santa Anna

San Cosme Causeway

Worth

Cathedral

Mexico City

Palace

Citadel

Chapultepec

Quitman

Tacubaya Causeway

Casa Mata

Worth

Pillow

Scott

Molino del Rey

Quitman

San Antonio Causeway

Twigg

0   1 mile

0   1 km

© Infobase Publishing   Tacubaya

how much of California each country would get, who paid for what war damages, whether Mexico would get any money for damages. Finally, the Mexicans asked Britain to guarantee the treaty. This was an astonishing and unusual request, especially since Britain and the United States had not that many years before fought against each other and had nearly come to blows over Oregon. Trist, after three days, rejected this condition. Santa Anna's government refused to negotiate further.

"And now, alas, we have all our fighting to do all over again," said Capt. Ephraim Smith, one of Scott's officers. Spies slipped into camp at twilight to inform Scott that at El Molino del Rey, the Mexicans were recasting church bells as cannon. It was also, they whispered, where the largest of the city's grain stores were kept. Hoping to disrupt production and destroy the city's food supply, Scott ordered General Worth to bombard the area with artillery. Forming into textbook columns, Worth's troops marched toward Casa Mata, the main structure, a powder magazine and a hornet's nest of four Mexican guns. It cost the U.S. forces some 700 casualties—dead and wounded—to take that small area.

After considering the best route to enter Mexico City, Scott decided to go in by the west approach, which meant that he first had to confront the Mexican army at the fortress of Chapultepec—then a summer palace, now the Mexican military academy—a little northeast of Tacubaya. On September 13, following a day and a half of heavy artillery bombardment, U.S. forces (numbering about 7,000) advanced; after only 90 minutes of close fighting, the Americans controlled Chapultepec—but with 500 men killed, wounded, or missing in action. Afterward, Colonel Hitchcock wrote in his diary, "We were like Pyrrhus after the fight with Fabricius—a few more victories and this army would be destroyed." (Pyrrhus was an ancient Greek warrior whose victory over the Romans at too high a cost inspired the phrase "Pyrrhic victory.")

Sensing that Mexico City now was within his grasp, Scott almost immediately ordered his troops to charge along the causeways leading into the city. Within hours, an American flag was flying over a section of the city's outer wall; next followed a bloody battle to take the inner city; at one point, Lt. Ulysses Grant mounted a howitzer in a church belfry to rain fire upon the Mexicans still in the streets and fighting the Americans.

One group of young Mexican officer cadets fought a losing, last-stand battle against the invaders. When it became clear that the

On September 13, 1847, U.S. forces stormed the last fortress standing between them and Mexico City: Chapultepec. Both sides suffered many casualties, but once the Mexicans surrendered, they realized that they could no longer defend Mexico City. (Library of Congress)

On September 14, 1847, General Scott led his troops on a triumphal entry into Mexico City to accept the surrender of the Mexicans and raise the U.S. flag in the Zócalo, the grand plaza in the center of the city. *(Library of Congress)*

norteamericanos had won that September 13, six of these teenage cadets committed suicide rather than live under the conquerors. They are forever known in the annals of Mexican history as Los Niños Heroes, or the Child Heroes. Francisco Márquez, Agustín Melgar, Juan Escutia, Fernando Montes de Oca, Vicente Suárez, and Juan de la Barrera came to symbolize the injustice of the war to the Mexicans.

On September 14, 1847, U.S. troops officially occupied Mexico City, although some street fighting and individual acts of violence went on for several weeks. U.S. forces had absorbed thousands of casualties in the campaign to take Mexico City, and the Mexicans had many thousands more. The best that can be said for such losses is that they put an end to what may have been even worse. The hostilities that had commenced in April 1846 seemed finally to have halted.

WEAPONS AND TACTICS

When on May 8, 1846, 2,288 U.S. soldiers under Brig. Gen. Zachary "Old Rough and Ready" Taylor were confronting that large force of Mexican soldiers at Palo Alto, they were beginning a war that would drastically change the map of a continent and the history of two nations.

The Mexican force was almost three times the size of the U.S. force. According to the *Lone Star Internet,* "Furthermore, Mexican troops were well armed, disciplined, and, above all, experienced in scores of revolutions." They certainly were experienced in revolutions. But they were "well armed" with mostly worn-out British "Brown Bess" muskets dating from the American Revolutionary War. They got no marksmanship training because the officers were afraid that too much shooting would make their muskets totally unusable. The Mexican troops had been poorly trained, were poorly motivated, and their only discipline was based on fear.

Mexico had achieved its independence from Spain 25 years earlier. Unlike the British colonies to the north, the Spanish colonies had had no semblance of self-rule. With independence, Mexico had been ruled by an emperor and a succession of presidents who were mostly successful revolutionaries. The Mexican troops were peons—peasants and unskilled laborers—who had been drafted for six-year terms.

Neither did U.S. troops came from high on the social scale. About 42 percent of them were penniless immigrants, half of them Irish, who could find no other work but the army. Discipline was ferocious, especially under "Old Rough and Ready." But the troops did get training, especially in marksmanship and drill.

To Europeans, both the United States and Mexico were semibarbaric ex-colonies. But within six years, Europeans at the Great

THE NAPOLÉON OF THE WEST

According to an old adage, you can't keep a good man down. Whether he was a good man or not is for Mexicans to decide, but Antonio de Padua María Severino López de Santa Anna y Pérez de Lebrón would certainly not be kept down. Known to Mexicans as "The Eagle"—and to himself as "The Napoléon of the West"—his career as a soldier and politician presents an almost unbelievable tale of resilience.

Santa Anna joined the Spanish army as a cadet at the age of 16. He became an officer and spent the next decade fighting insurgents and Indian tribes, during which he was wounded by an Indian arrow and cited for bravery. Keeping order in Mexico at that time was quite a job: The colony extended from Panama in the south to Oregon in the north. The declining Spanish Empire was not up to it. Santa Anna established a village for displaced persons near Veracruz and was seen as a champion of the poor and oppressed. The experience may have led him to sympathize with the rebels. Or perhaps he just saw more opportunity on the other side.

In 1821, Santa Anna joined the rebels. He was something they needed badly—a good tactician. He immediately drove the Spanish out

(continues)

This U.S. cartoon conveys the intensity of anti-Mexican feeling in the United States by depicting Generals Santa Anna and Perfecto de Cos surrendering abjectly to Samuel Houston after their defeat at the Battle of San Jacinto in April 1836. *(Library of Congress)*

(continues)

of Veracruz. The rebel leader, Augustín de Iturbide, made him a general. Santa Anna became known as the "Hero of Veracruz," and he looked like a hero. Only 30 years old, he was tall and handsome and identified himself with the common people, who adored him.

A year after Iturbide—now Emperor Augustín—made him a general, Santa Anna joined the republicans who wanted to overthrow Iturbide. The countries now forming Central America broke away from Mexico, and Iturbide went into exile. Santa Anna became one of the republican leaders who made and unmade presidents. After overthrowing two, Santa Anna was called upon to again save Mexico from Spain. Leading a much smaller force, he defeated a Spanish invasion force at Tampico in 1829.

Santa Anna retired to his hacienda, but then Anastasio Bustamante led a coup and made himself president. Santa Anna led the rebellion against Bustamante and was elected president in 1833. In the next three decades, Santa Anna would become his country's chief executive no less than seven times; he would be both the leader and the target of coups and rebellions; his status would vary from prisoner to "president for life." After one rebellion, he fled to the hills and was captured by cannibal Indians, who remembered his brutalities during his wars against Native American tribes. According to one version of the story, the Indians were heating up the stew pot when Santa Anna's enemies rescued him and clapped him into prison.

Santa Anna began his political career as a champion of democracy and autonomy for the Mexican states, but once in power, he favored highly centralized government with almost all power in the hands of the president. Santa Anna once stated his basic political principle: "Were I made God, I should wish to be something more."

Exhibition of 1851 in London would be marveling at what they called the "American System" of manufacturing. It was based on producing interchangeable parts and producing them with machine tools. The "American System" was first applied to gun manufacture. One reason was that there were few old-school master gunsmiths in the new country. Another was that all the practically free land in the United States induced people to go into farming instead of manufacturing. Lacking plentiful labor, the manufacturers opted for machinery. Production of manufactured items—especially machinery—increased tremendously.

There was no doubt that he had charisma. After years of broken promises, perfidy, and outright treachery, he was able to raise an army whenever he needed to. He demonstrated repeatedly that he was a good tactician, but he had huge military weaknesses. On the march, he kept loads of luxuries and uniforms gleaming with gold and gems but made almost no effort to make sure his troops had enough to eat, usable weapons, or sufficient ammunition.

When he set out for the Alamo, 365 miles away in San Antonio, Texas, it was January 26, 1836—the depth of winter on the high plateau he had to cross. Santa Anna and his personal bodyguard were not well equipped to cross the north-central desert, where there was little fodder for the horses and mules and the plateau was scoured by ferocious blizzards. Scores of troops from tropical places such as the Yucatán froze to death. Animals hauling supplies starved to death, leaving Santa Anna's poorly supplied army even more impoverished. He made no effort to keep the army together. Some of his troops did not reach San Antonio until after the Alamo had fallen.

Santa Anna's march discipline did not improve when he was pursuing Sam Houston and his Texans. As it had during his march through northern Mexico, much of his army dribbled away as it crossed Texas. Vain and overconfident as ever, Santa Anna camped in front of the Texans and ordered a siesta, setting up the massacre at San Jacinto.

Back in Mexico, he was deposed and exiled, but 10 years later, in August 1846, he was still able to persuade James Polk to return him to Mexico with a promise that he would regain power and make a peace favorable to the United States. Instead, immediately on arriving in Mexico City, he announced he was ready to lead the Mexican army against the U.S. forces. Santa Anna had bounced back again.

In 1840, the United States had more steamships than the entire British Empire and more railroad miles than all of Europe.

The United States was on the cutting edge of the Industrial Revolution—not yet the equal of Britain but far ahead of the rest of the world. Its army, though, did not reflect the importance of a rising industrial power. It was designed merely to keep order among Indian tribes and was only a quarter of the size of Mexico's. The United States spent little on the army. But in weaponry, tactics, and professionalism, the U.S. regular army was light-years ahead of Mexico's. Many of the American soldiers had smoothbore flintlocks, but many of the flintlocks were rifles, and one type, the Hall Rifle, was a breech-loading flintlock. There were also percussion rifles. But the most effective unit of the American military establishment was the light artillery, also called the "flying artillery" or the "horse artillery."

The light artillery guns dated only from 1840. The guns were mounted on carriages designed for towing at high speeds, and all of the gunners rode horses along with the guns. The prime piece of horse artillery in the Mexican-American War was the six-pounder. It was a gun (an artillery piece with a flatter trajectory than a howitzer or a mortar) and fired solid cannon balls, canister shot (a tin cylinder that broke up on leaving the muzzle and spraying hundreds of small balls like an enormous shotgun), explosive shells, and "spherical canister," what we now call shrapnel. It fired "fixed ammunition": in other words, a projectile attached to a bag containing the propelling charge. Loading was quick. The propelling charge was set off by a friction primer—a hollow spike containing a composition like an old-fashioned "strike anywhere" match. The gunner pulled a cord attached to a roughened

This cartoon depicts General Taylor at the Battle of Buena Vista in February 1847 at the moment when he is supposed to have shouted to his artillery chief, "A little more grape, Captain Bragg!" A "grape" is a type of shell formed with several balls bound together that burst on hitting the target. *(Library of Congress)*

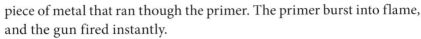

piece of metal that ran though the primer. The primer burst into flame, and the gun fired instantly.

The little six-pounder could not only fire faster than any artillery in the Mexican Army, it could outrange most of it. Until this type of horse artillery was introduced in the U.S.-Mexican War, military men had generally considered artillery a defensive arm. Brevet Maj. Samuel Ringgold at the artillery school at Fortress Monroe had trained his horse artillery to gallop to a position within range of the enemy, jump off their horses, and open fire as quickly as possible. He made the light artillery a breakthrough weapon. Many contemporary military observers considered the U.S. light artillery the best in the world. Ringgold was no mere theoretician. He led a horse artillery battery at the Battle of Palo Alto, where he was killed.

The Americans had guns heavier than those in the horse artillery, of course, but the fast-moving rapid-firing guns were the most spectacular. All of the artillery was the product of an effort in the 1830s and 1840s to modernize the U.S. artillery, which included the 12-, 18- and 24-pounder guns as well as the eight-pounders; the eight-inch and 24-pounder howitzers, and the eight- and 10-inch mortars. The Mexicans had nothing that could compare with any of them. The impact of the American artillery was obvious from the beginning, when the Mexicans were defeated almost solely by the horse artillery at Palo Alto. Artillery's potency continued to be demonstrated, especially at Buena Vista, and then again at Cerro Gordo, where young Capt. Robert E. Lee had his troops silently haul their 24-pounders by rope to the crest of a hill in order to surprise the Mexicans.

It was at Buena Vista that Santa Anna, having a huge advantage in manpower, managed to outmaneuver Taylor, who was not the brightest star in the U.S. military firmament, and get part of his army behind the U.S. forces. When darkness fell on the second day, Santa Anna's troops were poised in the rear of Taylor's army, and an attack the next morning could have been devastating. But the Mexican troops left their camp fires burning and slipped away. Santa Anna said his army had deserted him. Others say Santa Anna fled first. But whether or not the general lost his nerve before his troops, much of the responsibility for the resulting defeat belongs to the American artillery, which had punished the Mexicans severely.

The American gunners came up with new ways to use their artillery. During hand-to-hand fighting in urban areas, they lit the fuses of artillery shells and threw them into enemy positions as if they were hand grenades.

The Hall rifle was also used in a way never intended by its inventor, U.S. Army captain John H. Hall. Adopted by the U.S. Army in 1819, the Hall was a revolutionary breech-loader in an era of muzzle-loaders. Not only did it have a breech-loading mechanism, it had a detachable breech section containing the flintlock and trigger as well as the breech. Troops on leave in Mexican villages carried loaded Hall breeches in their pockets and used them as pistols. At least one veteran reported that he held off a hostile crowd in a cantina with his Hall breech.

In spite of its antiquated flintlock, the Hall was a fine weapon. First, it was a rifle, so the spiral grooves inside the barrel gave the bullet stability, which meant that it was accurate at a range far beyond anything possible with a smoothbore. The trouble with most rifles until this time was that they were slow to load. For the spiral grooves to do their work, the bullet had to be a tight fit. So even though the bullet was wrapped in a greased patch, seating it was slow work. But with the Hall, the shooter put the powder and bullet in the tilted-up breech section and snapped it closed. One did not have to force the bullet though the rifling. The Hall's breech did leak a bit of gas when it fired, but that was a minor inconvenience.

Another invention that made loading a rifle faster was what the troops called the "minié ball." This was a hollow-base bullet invented by Capt. Charles-Claude-Étienne Minié of the French army. It was smaller than the bore of the rifle, so loading a minié rifle was as quick as loading a muzzle loader, but when the gun was fired the cavity at the base of the bullet expanded to fit the rifling. Most rifles using the minié bullet had the percussion lock, which, instead of a flintlock, had a copper cap mounted on a nipple above the breech. The cap was filled with fulminate of mercury, and when the lock's hammer struck the cap, the fulminate exploded and fired the gun. The percussion cap was immensely more reliable than the flintlock.

Cavalry also played a significant role during the Mexican War. Many cavalrymen carried Sam Colt's revolutionary revolver. All cavalrymen carried the Model 1840 saber. This sword was so satisfactory that horsemen were still using it during the Civil War (1861–65). It was an excellent weapon for those trained to use it. However, recruits in both wars called it "the old wrist-breaker." Fledgling troopers practiced swinging it on horseback until, as one Civil War vet, Samuel H.

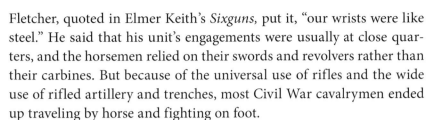

Fletcher, quoted in Elmer Keith's *Sixguns,* put it, "our wrists were like steel." He said that his unit's engagements were usually at close quarters, and the horsemen relied on their swords and revolvers rather than their carbines. But because of the universal use of rifles and the wide use of rifled artillery and trenches, most Civil War cavalrymen ended up traveling by horse and fighting on foot.

The revolver got its start in the Mexican War. Samuel Colt had actually invented his pistol 14 years earlier, and it saw much service during the Texas war for independence and the U.S. war against the Seminole Indians. But when the fighting stopped, the demand for revolvers dropped too. And the financial mismanagement of Colt's associates drove the Patent Arms Manufacturing Company into bankruptcy. When the new trouble with Mexico erupted, Captain Samuel H. Walker of the Texas Rangers tried to get another order of revolvers, but Colt was out of business. Colt made an arrangement with another gun maker, Eli Whitney, Jr., who pioneered interchangeable parts in the manufacture of the "Mississippi rifle," one of the country's newest infantry rifles, to use the facilities of his factory.

Walker, who was praised by General Taylor for his conduct at Palo Alto and Resaca de la Palma and for "very meritorious service as a spy and a partisan," visited Colt with suggestions for a new revolver. Colt could not find a sample of one of his previous revolvers, but he designed a new one largely from memory and according to Walker's suggestions. The result was the Walker Colt, a gun adopted by the army and used for years after the war in the opening of the West. The Walker Colt was a huge weapon—about the size of the modern .44 magnum and more powerful than any modern non-magnum revolver. Colt's fortune was made, and revolvers became the preferred handgun of militaries around the world.

Captain Walker did not survive the war with Mexico. He was killed by a Mexican lancer in the state of Tlaxcala during Scott's march across Mexico. Lancers were a medieval military arm that had almost disappeared in Europe before Napoléon revived them. He had been impressed with the Polish lancers he encountered, and since most European nations were impressed with Napoléon, they organized their own lancer regiments. Lancers never caught on in the United States, but they were an important part of Latin American armies, even—or especially—revolutionary guerrilla outfits. The lance was a weapon ideally suited to an impoverished military. It was far less costly than a

At Medelín, on the outskirts of Veracruz, Col. William S. Harney, a cavalry officer from Tennessee, led his troops in a hard-fought, close-quarters battle on March 25, 1847. Note that the U.S. cavalrymen are using the heavy swords known as "wrist-breakers," while the Mexicans are using lances—both weapons that soldiers had used for many centuries. *(Library of Congress)*

revolver, being merely a blade on the end of a pole. It required almost no maintenance, and for an accomplished horseman, as many Latinos were, it required little training.

No Latino horsemen—or horsemen of any other ethnic group—were more accomplished than the Californios, the indolent, hospitable, and gracious ranchers in what is now the U.S. state of California. The Californios kept hundreds of horses, unfenced and unhobbled. Each horse had a long rope around its neck that trailed behind it. The Californio would simply grab the rope of the horse he wanted and pull the animal over to be saddled. According to Richard Henry Dana, a Californio would walk a mile to get a horse to ride half that distance.

On December 6, 1846, Gen. Stephen Kearny, approaching San Diego, saw a party of mounted Californios near the village of San Pascual. They were carrying lances, but U.S. Marine lieutenant Archibald Gillespie, who had been in California several months, and mountain man Kit Carson told Kearny that they were only Californios and would not fight.

Kearny ordered a charge. The fight lasted only a few minutes. When it was over, 18 Americans were dead and the Californios rode away with one of Kearny's two howitzers, after handing U.S. troops their only defeat in the war with Mexico.

A pistol, though, could always outrange a lance, and a revolver like the Colt made one man with a pistol the equal of six lancers. Some troops carried two or more revolvers, and others carried several loaded cylinders: They could quickly replace cylinders that became empty. But in war, even the best armaments have no guarantee. There is always the element of luck. At Tlaxcala, Captain Walker's had run out.

In the Mexican War, the Americans carried one unofficial weapon widely—the bowie knife. It was probably more useful for household chores such as cutting rope, carving tent pegs, or preparing food than for fighting Mexicans, but its availability undoubtedly comforted the soldier who carried it. Most bayonets in those days, while attached to a musket or rifle, were not much use for anything except stabbing. A bowie knife was a more effective weapon in a hand-to-hand fight, as it proved to be at the Battle of Buena Vista. And many of the troops had probably used it for fighting before they even joined the army.

The five-day bombardment of Veracruz in March 1847 from both sailing ships and steamships, as well as from onshore artillery, was one of the heaviest and most destructive such actions in military history to that point. (*Library of Congress*)

JIM THE KNIFE

James Bowie was a prosperous Louisiana planter and land speculator, a member of what was later called the "Bowie knife and pistol gentry." Like other members of his class in the Old Southwest, young Jim was a trifle "tetchy," and made some enemies. One of them, Major Norris Wright, shot him. After that, Jim's brother, Rezin, thought Jim's two single-shot pistols might not be enough protection for him, so he gave him a duplicate of a knife he had used to save himself from a mad bull.

Although there are several variations on the so-called bowie knife, this is probably the standard. The blade could be from six to 12 inches long and is characterized by a "clip point," the dip in the forward part of the blade that makes a sharper point. *(Private collection)*

Rezin was right. Jim was asked to be a second for his friend Samuel Wells, who had been challenged to a duel. Duels in the Old Southwest did not resemble the ritualistic Burr-Hamilton affair. They were more like armed mob fights. Wells had a crowd of seconds. So did his opponent. One of the opponent's seconds was Bowie's old enemy Major Norris Wright. Wright shot Bowie in the leg, and while Jim was on the ground, tried to stab him with a sword cane. Bowie wriggled away and sat up. His pistols were empty, but he reached under his coat, drew his knife, and killed Wright with one stroke.

The U.S.-Mexican War was fought entirely on land, but the U.S. Navy played a vital role, carrying troops and supplies, blockading large stretches of the Mexican coast, and providing bombardments for several major coastal actions. In what was a first in any war, the navy used steamships to carry troops and supplies along American rivers and from U.S. ports to Mexican ports. In particular, the navy set the stage for the key campaign in the war by capturing Tampico and then Veracruz, which Scott used as the base for his march across Mexico. Scott was not able to land his heavy siege guns immediately, so he relied

This "Vidalia Sandbar Fight"—it took place on a Mississippi sand-bar near Vidalia, Louisiana—commanded a lot of attention and news-paper space. For some reason, the knife seemed to get as much credit for the outcome as the knife wielder. Men everywhere wanted "a knife like Bowie's," although few even knew what it looked like. Bowie seems to have given the Vidalia knife to Edwin Forrest, and it may be that he had another made by James Black, the Arkansas blacksmith.

Like the traditional gunfighter of Wild West movies, Bowie became a target for would-be tough guys. One was a Natchez gambler named Sturdivant, who challenged Bowie to a fight. The left arms of the two fighters were tied together, and each held his knife in his right hand. Sturdivant attacked; Bowie parried and reposted, cutting the tendons in the gambler's arm. Bowie spared Sturdivant's life and traveled to Texas, where he bought land, became a citizen, and married a Mexican woman. On his return to Natchez, he was said to have been attacked by three knife-wielding thugs hired by Sturdivant. With his new knife, it is claimed that he decapitated the thug who seized his bridle, dismounted and disemboweled the second assassin, then chased and split the skull of the third.

The carnage Bowie wrought with his new knife indicates that it was a pretty big, heavy weapon. Like many semilegendary characters, it is hard to tell which stories about Bowie are true, which are greatly exag-gerated, and which are pure fiction. It is certain, however, that Bowie joined the defenders of the Alamo and that he became seriously ill and was confined to his bed when the Mexicans broke in. He was firing at them with his pistols when the Mexican troops speared him and lifted him up on their bayonets "until his blood covered their clothes and dyed them red," in the words of his horrified sister-in-law, Juana Veramendi de Alsbury. But Bowie's name lived on in the knife.

on the guns of the navy's fleet of windjammers and steamships to bom-bard the heavily fortified city of Veracruz. Scott's army then performed the first American amphibious assault with specially designed assault boats, but he did not land under fire. He did not believe in risking his men unnecessarily, so he landed on beaches out of range of the guns in Veracruz's forts. Then he began to lay siege before he got his heavy guns ashore. While ships' guns were bombarding Veracruz, Scott's engineers, who included Robert E. Lee, George B. McClellan, P. T. G. Beauregard, and Joseph Johnston (all future Civil War generals), dug parallel trenches and approach trenches around the city and positioned batteries in a way that would have met the approval of Sébastien le Prestre de Vauban, the great 18th-century French engineer. Veracruz surrendered in 20 days. Scott lost only 69 men. Earlier, the navy had played a major role in the somewhat comic-opera conquest of California, which featured a Mexican governor, Pío Pico, who was not all that opposed to annexation by the United States, and the somewhat bogus Bear Flag Republic.

Whatever the role of the U.S. Navy, the American soldiers' and sailors' weapons and their skill in using them made the U.S.-Mexican War one of this country's more one-sided conflicts as well as its most profitable. In addition to new weapons and skills, the United States also employed new technologies that prefigured the nature of warfare to come. The use of steamships has been mentioned; the railroad was used to move troops and supplies through regions of the United States; the telegraph was used to speed up communications. And although not an advantage to the military, photographs (based on the daguerreotype) and newspaper reporters traveling with the troops gave civilians at home a clearer sense of the progress of the war. In the end, Mexico was simply unable to match the technologies, weapons, and tactics of the United States.

10

"WE TAKE NOTHING BY CONQUEST, BY GOD!"

The winding down of the Mexican War proved to be as tangled, bungled, and drawn-out as the gearing up had been. All the problems that had plagued the war from the beginning—politics and personalities, logistics and communications, egotism and honor—all this and more continued to drag out its ending.

As soon as it was clear that the U.S. forces were going to take over Mexico City, early that morning of September 14, 1847, Santa Anna gathered a few hundred of his troops and made his way out of the city. After a brief stopover at the town of Guadalupe Hidalgo, he decided entirely on his own to mount a counterattack by capturing Puebla, just east of Mexico City. Then Mexico's second largest city, Puebla had been held by U.S. soldiers since April. On September 25, Santa Anna arrived at Puebla, claiming a force of 8,000 men gathered along the way. Defiant, his pride stung by the loss of the capital, Santa Anna and his supporters sent a messenger forward with a white flag flapping in one hand, and in his other hand a message for the U.S. commander in charge within Puebla, Col. Thomas Childs. Childs refused to give in to Mexican demands for surrender. The Mexicans responded with a siege: no pitched battles, just a slow squeeze on food, water, and firewood. Every day the pressure mounted. A few soldiers fired a round of ammunition here and there—just enough to harass, not enough to fully engage the city's defenders.

But weeks before Santa Anna had placed Puebla under siege, 1,000 U.S. soldiers were struggling through the highlands between Veracruz and Jalapa. Despite fever and bandits, they had been doing so since

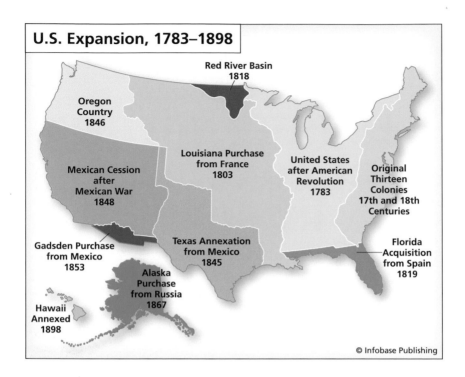

U.S. Expansion, 1783–1898

Red River Basin
1818

Oregon
Country
1846

Louisiana Purchase
from France
1803

United States
after American
Revolution
1783

Original
Thirteen
Colonies
17th and 18th
Centuries

Mexican Cession
after
Mexican War
1848

Gadsden Purchase
from Mexico
1853

Texas Annexation
from Mexico
1845

Alaska
Purchase
from Russia
1867

Florida
Acquisition
from Spain
1819

Hawaii
Annexed
1898

© Infobase Publishing

August 6, with the original assignment to support Scott's attack on
Mexico City. Then, in September, a new regiment (numbering about
800) caught up with them; they were fresh from the States. Then came
another, then two more regiments from Taylor's old army in northern
Mexico. Joining at Jalapa, a total of 4,000 U.S. troops marched toward
Puebla under Brig. Gen. Joseph Lane. Santa Anna made one final effort
to mount a challenge with about 2,500 troops and six pieces of artillery,
but his soldiers fled, and Lane and his men went on to relieve Puebla
on October 6.

In the meantime, Santa Anna had been forced to resign the presidency and on September 26, Manuel Peña y Peña, the moderate chief
justice of Mexico, wearily took over as president of Mexico. He did not
want the job, yet there he was, under oath to begin a peace process for
the war that, in 1845, he had tried so hard to avoid. Perhaps his most
difficult task at first was to deal with Santa Anna, who was conducting
the unauthorized siege at Puebla. The "wily chameleon," at last was
ordered to turn over his command and wait until his conduct—always
a little suspicious—could be investigated. But, protested the general,
he was being sacrificed to make an "inglorious peace" with the North

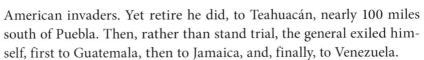

American invaders. Yet retire he did, to Teahuacán, nearly 100 miles south of Puebla. Then, rather than stand trial, the general exiled himself, first to Guatemala, then to Jamaica, and, finally, to Venezuela.

In October 1847, however, even with the mercurial Santa Anna out of the way, the Mexican government remained disorganized and confused about what to do next. On the one hand, its sovereignty seemed to be guaranteed. But over how much territory? Were Mexicans in a state of truce, a state of siege, or total occupation? Could they say no to what the enemy offered them, with that enemy lodged in the heart of their government, the capital itself? (The government had temporarily settled in a city north of Mexico City, Queretaro.) Gómez Farías, the old liberal reformer, reappeared long enough to cry for release from the greedy *gringos*—no peace proposals until the enemy removed himself from Mexican territory! He also called for getting rid of Peña y Peña, whom he regarded as the North Americans' puppet.

Mexican congressmen met into long hours of the night. The U.S. military delegates stepped briskly in and out of the houses and patios of important congressmen. Long after the North Americans left, their unfortunate hosts sat under the eaves of their courtyards, looking into the shadows. In the halls of Mexico's congress, fistfights nearly broke out over Gómez Farías's resolution, yet everyone knew that the North Americans were virtually ready to declare both sides irrelevant. The resolution was defeated 38 to 35. A pacifist proposal also went nowhere. About all the congress could accomplish was, on November 11, to select a successor to Peña y Peña, one Pedro María Anaya. Some historians have suggested that Anaya was in fact a U.S. puppet, for after he was sworn in, Anaya turned right around and asked Peña y Peña to serve as his minister of foreign affairs so the negotiations could go on without interruption.

In the meantime, the North Americans, whether in Washington or Mexico, were not conducting their affairs much more rationally. On October 6, President Polk had received word of how Trist had negotiated with the Mexicans during the Armistice of Tacubaya—that temporary delay on the road to Mexico City, August 24 to September 6. Polk got up out of his sickbed in a rage and issued an order recalling Trist; Polk even repeated this order some two weeks later. Undoubtedly, part of Polk's anger stemmed from his fear that Trist would bargain away his beloved California. Did Polk want the whole of Mexico, as some North Americans were now beginning to demand? Perhaps not, but certainly he wanted California.

It was November 16 before Trist received clear instructions from Washington to step down. Peña y Peña had just taken over as foreign minister, and when he heard that Trist had been fired, he realized that Polk and his Washington crowd were undoubtedly planning much harsher terms than anything Trist had demanded. Peña y Peña and the Mexican government joined General Scott and the British delegation in urging Trist to stay on and conduct the final peace negotiations. On December 4, after careful deliberations, Trist decided to ignore Polk's order. As the second-highest ranking member of the U.S. State Department, he would proceed to work out a peace treaty based on his own understanding of the situation. On December 6, he wrote a letter to justify his decision to his boss, Secretary of State James Buchanan, explaining that, "if the present opportunity be not seized *at once,* all chance of making a treaty *at all* will be lost for an indefinite period—probably forever."

Trist's letter rambled on and on, though with a certain reasonableness. Then he wrote down what later infuriated Polk: "Infallibility of judgment . . . is not among the attributes of a President of the United States, even when his sentences rest upon full & accurate knowledge of all the facts." It hardly needed a translator to see that Trist did not think much of Polk's judgment about diplomatic matters. After making a few snide remarks about General Pillow, "Polk's Spy," Trist signed his long dispatch, blotted the ink and called for a messenger. Off Trist's letter went but, as he probably knew, it would not reach Washington for several weeks. Having sent this, Trist then chose not to communicate again with his government for the next two months.

In the United States, meanwhile, the temper was changing, and there was now a growing movement to impose harsh terms on Mexico. Since Scott's victory, public opinion seemed to have changed. No longer just "Mr. Polk's War," Scott's victory turned it into a glorious opportunity to double U.S. possessions. In his December 1847 annual address, President Polk justified taking Mexican land in the strangest way: Polk argued that if the United States did not ask for territory, it would be admitting it should not have started the war. He then went on to urge that California and New Mexico be annexed because Mexico was too weak to govern these two northern Mexican states. Polk then dropped a hint that drove the expansionists wild with enthusiasm: Perhaps the United States should take all of Mexico as a protectorate—basically, continue U.S. presence in Mexico—if the country continued to be so unstable.

"[M]ake General Scott Governor of the Whole," responded the Philadelphia *Public Ledger* enthusiastically to the protectorate idea, "allow it three or four delegates in Congress; open it to emigration from the United States and Europe . . . Our Yankee young fellows and the pretty señoritas will do the rest of the annexation, and Mexico will soon be Anglo-Saxonized and prepared for the confederacy."

Victory had gone straight to the heads of the United States politicians as well as some of their constituents. Why not take all of Mexico? some now asked. Even James Buchanan, Polk's secretary of state, had started to consider taking over all of the northern states of Mexico, possibly—why not?—the whole country. Actually, Buchanan had presidential stars in his eyes and he did not want to scare away expansionist votes. And it looked like annexation fever was going to dominate the coming election, because every Democrat seeking election made mention of the patriotic benefits of putting Mexico in Uncle Sam's back pocket. The British and the French thought the United States would be crazy to take on such a large area with a population so diverse.

In the midst of this Mexican annexation fever sweeping the United States, on January 2, 1848, Trist began formal negotiations with Mexico. On January 4, Polk found out that Trist was still negotiating, and on January 15, Polk received word of Trist's long and arrogant letter refusing to stop. Trist continued dickering with the Mexican commissioners until on January 31 the Mexican government, still temporarily installed at Queretaro, sent a messenger to Mexico City with a message saying that they, the current Mexican authorities, were in agreement with the terms of the treaty. Either their anxiety or their enthusiasm must have been high: The messenger rode the 150 miles in less than two days. Trist and the Mexican commissioners signed the treaty in the small village of Guadalupe Hidalgo on the afternoon of February 2, 1848.

Depending on where the characterizer's sympathies lie, the terms that Trist agreed to have been characterized as too generous to the United States, too generous to Mexico, or just about what both could have expected. Texas, of course, was once and for all recognized as belonging to the United States; the boundary between the two countries was set to follow the Rio Grande up from the Gulf to El Paso, cut westward at about 32° latitude, along the Gila River to the Colorado River, and then due west to the Pacific Coast. The vast provinces of New Mexico and California were turned over to the United States for only $15 million. Those were goals that many Americans sought. But Trist also agreed that the United States should assume payment of the claims owed to its citizens by Mexico (which came to more than $7 million); he agreed that the United States should assume the costs for claims made by Mexican citizens against Indians from the United States (which came to some $31 million); he failed to gain an outlet for the United States on the Gulf of California and to obtain a good railroad route across the Southwest to the Pacific Coast; and he conceded various other rights to Mexicans living in what would now be U.S. territory. Perhaps the final tribute to Trist's treaty is the classic one, that extremists on both sides, then and later, regarded it as a sellout.

Trist sent his treaty to Washington with the help of a war correspondent, James L. Freaner, of the New Orleans *Delta*. With a news scoop in one hand and the treaty in the other, Freaner arrived in the capital on Saturday night, February 19. "[C]ontemptibly base!" sputtered Polk, referring to his ex-agent who, it seems, had negotiated a treaty that Polk was then obliged to take to Congress and the Senate. In his diary the president blustered that Trist had "acted worse than any man in the public employ whom I have ever known." Yes, he got his beloved California, but there would be some in the Senate demanding still more.

And demand they did. As soon as the treaty came to the Senate, Sam Houston from Texas took the floor. Not enough land. This "Trist paper" did not take enough. Wrong, cried Daniel Webster of Massachusetts, who was "against all accessions of territory to form new states." Translated, that meant no new slave states. Jefferson Davis of Mississippi sprang to the floor: How about including Tamaulipas, Nuevo León, Coahuila; and Chihuahua, the northern tier of Mexico's states? But Trist, Daniel Webster, and the Whigs pointed out, was not a legal representative of the government. Why not send a new commission to Mexico to renegotiate the treaty legally? Mississippi's Robert J. Walker, secretary of the treasury, excitedly warned Polk that such a new commission was an anti-expansionist plot by Webster. Then John Quincy Adams, the Massachusetts representative who reluctantly voted for the war back in May 1846, had an actual stroke in the midst of these arguments and died two days later; this served to calm everyone down a bit. Walker and Secretary of State Buchanan scurried around Washington and into the rooms where deals were made. The *New*

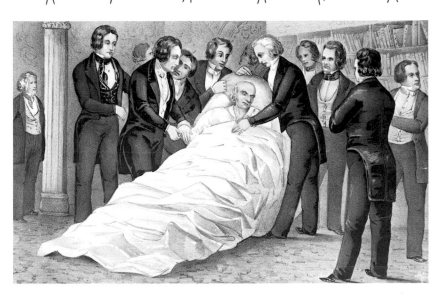

John Quincy Adams at the U.S. Capitol on February 23, 1848, after suffering a fatal stroke during Senate meetings on Nicholas Trist's proposed treaty (*Library of Congress*)

York Herald published some damaging correspondence regarding the Slidell and Trist missions, and that Polk and his cabinet knew would soon reach the Mexican press. When it did, Gómez Farías and his fellow purists would renew their opposition to the treaty. Perhaps Trist's treaty was not so bad after all.

Finally, Trist's treaty, with minor amendments, was ratified by the U.S. Senate on March 10, 1848. The vote was 38 to 14. A week later, Trist himself was arrested by the U.S. military in Mexico City and taken out of the country under guard; he never was put on trial, but it was 25 years before the U.S. government paid him for his expenses in negotiating this treaty. And he was forever branded by the expansionist-minded U.S. politicians as a scoundrel, even though his terms had resulted in acquisition of vast tracts of Mexican lands.

In May, Attorney General Nathan Clifford and Senator Ambrose Sevier, chair of the Senate Foreign Relations Committee, arrived in Querétaro to finalize the details of the treaty. On May 30, ratifications of the treaty were formally exchanged in Querétaro. At that time, the United States also gave $15 million for California and New Mexico, an act which caused one U.S. lawmaker to claim, "We take nothing by conquest, by God!" On June 5, the last shot of the war was fired in the

Baja California town of Todos Santos—by a New York regiment under General Wool.

Again and again, historians write of the relative thriftiness of the war: it cost "only" $100 million and some 15,000 lives (U.S. lives, that is; Mexican casualties—soldiers or civilians—were never officially counted but there must have been at least three or four times as many). Among the U.S. dead, 1,733 were either killed in battle or died from their wounds; the rest died of disease or exposure or they simply disappeared.

Ulysses S. Grant, who fought in the war, later said that "Scott's successes are the answer to all criticisms." Britain's duke of Wellington, victor over Napoléon, unequivocally called Scott's campaign "unsurpassed in military annals." And military historians agree that it was Scott's strategy and tactics that won battles and the war. Training had at best been perfunctory—especially where the volunteers were concerned—and discipline was frequently more honored in the breach; organization was often chaotic and logistics seemed improvised; officers' leadership was there when necessary and rank-and-file courage prevailed in the heat of battle. But it was with Scott's reliance on superior firepower that the Mexican War made grim history: It was a lesson that the U.S. military would not forget in the decades that followed.

Military accounting aside, the fact is that, in less than two years' time, the United States acquired almost half of Mexico. For $15 million dollars, plus the payments for those other claims, the United States increased its own lands by almost one-third (this is including Texas). Out of the new territory gained, the United States eventually created Nevada, New Mexico, Arizona, Utah, Wyoming, and parts of Kansas and Colorado. Through a later treaty, the 1853 Gadsden Purchase (so named after James Gadsden, the ambassador to Mexico who arranged it), for $10 million the United States bought close to 30,000 square miles more from Mexico, territory that became southern Arizona and southern New Mexico. This land was wanted to provide a better southern railroad route to the Pacific.

But the major prize was California. The whole country loved California. It particularly loved California when the gold rush began in 1848, right on the heels of victory. The United States, in fact, was so taken by California and the hope of getting rich quick that the poor Whig party, which had opposed the idea of Manifest Destiny, dwindled into nothing. The dream of gain had caught fire and consumed all

THE GADSDEN PURCHASE AND THE RAIL ROUTE

After the 1848 Treaty of Guadalupe Hidalgo ceded Texas and most of New Mexico, Arizona, California, Colorado, Utah, and Nevada, a sliver of land still in Mexico's possession became of great interest to one James Gadsden. Veteran of the Seminole Wars and a developer of railroads, Gadsden envisioned a transcontinental railway that would connect the South, not the North, with the West. As president of the South Carolina Railway, he saw that the most desirable route was below the then U.S. border, in Mexico. Nor was it lost upon him that silver and gold ore had been found in the area. By 1853, through Secretary of War Jefferson Davis, Gadsden finagled an appointment as U.S. ambassador to Mexico under President Franklin Pierce. Working on the president, Gadsden finally purchased a narrow strip of land south of the Gila River, part southern Arizona, part southwest New Mexico. The Treaty of Mesilla, named after the Mexican town where it was signed in 1854, closed Gadsden's purchase for $10 million. Eventually the Santa Fe Railway Company made its connection at Las Cruces, 3.5 miles farther north.

Only a week before the treaty was signed by which the United States acquired California from Mexico, gold was discovered there, leading to the famous "gold rush" that brought several hundred thousand people there. *(Library of Congress)*

opposition. Of course the issue of slavery did not go away—nor did economic insecurity—but these issues were left to fester a little longer while settlers raced to reach the lands of milk and honey in the West. The builders of railways and all those who would make their fortunes as the country was opened up by rail—they were hungry for the land that now lay before them in the new West. Yet even they could not anticipate the immense riches that lay buried within the former Mexican lands—the petroleum and minerals—nor the agricultural, touristic, and other resources that North Americans would one day be able to exploit in the former Nueva España.

It was in the heat and haze of a June morning in the Valley of Mexico, with the squeaking of wagons carrying heavy metal and weary soldiers, that the last of the North Americans left Mexico City for home. As armies inevitably seem to do—in this case, it was General Worth's regiment—they held a ceremony in the Grand Plaza of the capital. The Stars and Stripes fluttered on its way down the flagpole that stood in front of the Palacio Nacional, the government offices of Mexico. The Mexican eagle soared over the land once more, although that land was much smaller than before. Under this grand symbol of the bird of prey clutching the serpent, small hands fingered $3 million in coin, the first U.S. payment to the defeated nation. Shortly afterward, José Joaquín Herrera assumed the presidency. Santa Anna would return to Mexico in 1853 and again become its president; yet once again, he was forced into exile in 1855 and not allowed back until 1874; impoverished and disempowered, he survived another two years, one of Mexico's most flamboyant leaders.

Gen. Winfield Scott had sailed out of Veracruz in April, homeward bound as a conquering hero. Once home, though, due to political and personal machinations, Scott had to answer various charges in a court of inquiry ordered by President Polk. Scott was acquitted of any wrongdoing, but when he ran for president in 1852, he was defeated by a former army subordinate, Franklin Pierce.

James Polk, having enlarged his country by even more than he could have imagined, retired in 1849 after his one term, and just as he had feared, his war had "made" his successor—not General Scott but Gen. Zachary Taylor. Taylor was elected president in 1848 but died after only 16 months in office. Then in 1853, Franklin Pierce took over the presidency: Polk's war made not one, but two, war heroes into presidents—four, if James Buchanan and Jefferson Davis are so regarded.

Later, of course, Ulysses Grant would also become president, although that was due to his Civil War service.

As for any sense of glory that the war may have engendered in the troops who fought it, the reaction of the ordinary soldiers—many of them men who had come home maimed or so diseased that they soon died or spent their remaining years as war victims—was not pleasant. When the Massachusetts Volunteers came home to a reception in honor of their return, the men hissed their own commander, General Cushing. The local papers claimed that former recruits spoke darkly of all kinds of improper behavior on the part of their officers. The returning recruits suffered from lack of money and a difficult transition to civilian life, just as in the aftermath of the Vietnam War. While some were given land as a reward for service, claimed an article in New York's *Commercial Advertiser,* many sold the land to keep body and soul together:

> It is a well-known fact that immense fortunes were made out of the poor soldiers who shed their blood in the Revolutionary War by spectators who preyed upon their distress. A similar system . . . was practiced on the soldiers of the last [Mexican] war.

So, too, did many Mexicans lose their claim to lands in the U.S. territories where they remained. It is still possible to travel in places like New Mexico and find descendants of these original settlers who possess yellowed, fragile pieces of paper, written in colonial Spanish with great flourish, assuring their claim to lands no longer theirs. For Article X of the Trist document was not ratified by Congress. (This was one of the unintended results of Trist's "solo act" there in Mexico: Congress felt no obligation to ratify every term he negotiated.) What the unratified Article X gave was guarantees of "all prior and pending titles to property of every description." What was most important about this was the guarantee that their homes and land would not be taken from them. Mexicans living in conquered territory were reassured by a "Statement of Protocol" on May 26, 1848, which said that not voting for Article X "did not in any way intend to annul the grants of lands made by Mexico in the ceded territories." This document went on to specify the laws that gave the property grants in the first place; without such assurance, the Mexicans would never have signed the treaty. The promises have not always been kept.

A sharp attack by the Democrats in the 1848 presidential election, this cartoon represents either of the two potential Whig candidates, Gen. Winfield Scott and Gen. Zachary Taylor, sitting on a pyramid of Mexican skulls, suggesting that the casualties that they inflicted in the war are their only qualification. Taylor was nominated and won the election but died after serving only 16 months. *(Library of Congress)*

Under other provisions of the treaty, Mexicans in the seized territories could leave the United States—2,000 did—or stay. Most stayed on what they considered—erroneously, it seemed—their land. Article IX gave the remaining Mexicans "the enjoyment of all the rights of citizens of the United States according to the principles of the Constitution; and in the meantime shall be maintained and protected in the free enjoyment of their liberty and property, and secured in the free exercise of their religion without restriction." That is, they were given citizenship, the same rights as citizens till then, including the right to own land and worship freely.

But at the time the treaty was signed, Manuel Crescíon Rejón, the Mexican diplomat, remarked: "Descendants of the Indians that we are, the North Americans hate us, their spokesmen depreciate us, even if they recognize the justice of our cause, and they consider us unworthy to form with them one nation and one society, they clearly [show] that their future expansion begins with the territory that they take from us and pushing aside our citizens who inhabit the land." Some negative

SPANISH LAND GRANTS AND THE TRIST DOCUMENT

When Nicholas Trist disobeyed Polk's orders to cut off negotiations ending the war, defeated Mexican officials knew they needed to reach an agreement quickly, or suffer even more losses. In one month—from January 2 to February 2, 1848—Trist and Mexican representatives hammered out the Treaty of Guadalupe Hidalgo. On May 19, 1848, Congress ratified all but Article X: Polk got his beloved California, but expansionist hopes for taking all of Mexico were dashed.

Several articles of the Treaty of Guadalupe Hidalgo referred to the rights of Mexicans who now found themselves living in U.S. territory. If they wished to leave, they had a year in which to do so. Article IX guaranteed those who remained that, "all rights of citizens of the United States according to the principles of the Constitution . . . shall be maintained and protected in the free enjoyment of their liberty and property, and. . . . religion."

Article X of the treaty specifically honored prior Spanish land grants made to these new citizens, but Polk objected vehemently and Congress struck it down before ratification. Then, in 1848, the United States and Mexico Protocol of Querétero clarified Guadalupe Hidalgo's Article II, which said that rejecting Article X was not an annulment of land grant titles. The protocol reaffirmed that such rights of title would be protected; such claims could be acknowledged before U.S. tribunals. The Treaty of Mesilla, concluding the Gadsden Purchase (1854), also reaffirmed the property guarantees of Guadalupe Hidalgo.

In New Mexico, concern over Spanish land grants continued. Thus, in 1854, Congress established the Office of Surveyor General of New Mexico, which was specifically charged to review and verify all documents pertaining to land grant ownership. Sixty-four claims were approved by Congress, returning title to disputed property, but such activity stopped in the late 1870s. Since reactivation, a few hundred additional land grants have been confirmed but most await negotiation.

attitudes about Latinos in the United States survive to this day and hold many back from full participation in the country that they have chosen to live in. To that extent, the Mexican War has never ended for some.

Officially, though, the war ended in 1848. At that time, Polk made an ambitious claim: "Peace, plenty, and contentment reign throughout our borders, and our beloved country presents a sublime moral spectacle to the world." Before accepting that as the final word, consider a eulogy for the northern part of Mexico, delivered two years before by the acting governor of New Mexico, Juan Bautista Virgil y Alarid:

> The power of the Mexican Republic [in northern Mexico] is dead . . . No one in the world can resist the power of him who is stronger. Mexico had been our mother; it was only just that we should weep at her tomb.

In the end, that was what the Mexican War had been about. Call it Manifest Destiny or "historical inevitability" or the march of progress, the "power of him who is stronger" had prevailed.

Except for the wars waged to push the Native Americans off their lands, the Mexican War is perhaps the only war fought by the United States that has no other justification except the desire for more territory. Citizens of the United States would soon consider it impossible to imagine the former Mexican territory as anything except a part of their Union. Many Mexicans did not, and still do not, find this so unthinkable. Nor do glib allusions to "other times, other customs" totally fulfill the need for a nation to confront the realities of its own history.

In any case, it was not immediately and purely a bonanza, this great new territory. The issue that had been shadowing it from the outset—the question over whether slavery should be allowed in any new lands acquired by the United States—was now quickly moved into the spotlight by this new accession. Those who had been most in favor of the war with Mexico, principally the southern states, could not believe that all this new land had been acquired only to remain off limits to slaveholders. More and more North Americans were forced to choose sides on the slavery question as the concept of "popular sovereignty"—the notion that new territories and states should be able to choose slavery or not—replaced the Missouri Compromise of 1820. The immediate result was the Compromise of 1850 that the nation's responsible leaders worked out—allowing a bit to slavery here, foreclosing on a bit of slavery there—but this only postponed while aggravating the inevitable. No historian would claim that the acquisition of these Mexican lands caused the Civil War, any more than they would deny that the Civil War probably would have been fought even without the aggravations of the former Mexican territory. But some of the attitudes, the mood,

Today a fence separates large sections of the U.S.-Mexican border to prevent illegal entrants. The stretch seen here separates the densely populated Mexican city of Tijuana, right, from the U.S. sector, only 16 miles from downtown San Diego. *(Photo by Gordon Hyde/Department of Defense)*

the spirit released by the Mexican War and endorsed by its outcome may well have contributed to the divisiveness, extremism, and belligerence that brought about the Civil War. In that sense, Manifest Destiny exacted a heavy price.

One thing is certain: The Mexican War was the training ground for many of the most prominent military leaders in the Civil War, both Confederates and Federals, who fought side by side in the Mexican War. Drawing on this experience, they would be fighting and killing one another within 15 years of the victory over Mexico.

Glossary

amphibious operation   The landing of troops and equipment from the sea in boats or vehicles that can move into shallow water; the vehicles are able to travel up onto the beach.

Anglo   When added to other terms, meaning "English" or, most commonly, "North American." For example, "Anglo-Texans" are Texans from the United States, and "Anglo–Nuevo Mexicanos" are New Mexicans of the United States. The term is sometimes shortened to "Anglos." It is derived from Anglo-Saxon, long a label for the dominant ancestry of many English-speaking northern Europeans.

annexation   To incorporate by force or administrative decision a territory or political unit into another political unit. The word *annexationist* first entered the U.S. vocabulary in 1845 with the debate on annexing the Republic of Texas.

armchair strategist   A disparaging term referring to the nonmilitary individuals who plan wars from the safety of their armchairs, usually in Washington, D.C.

atrocity   A particularly savage or brutal action, especially one carried out during a war and often involving the killing of innocent civilians. Precise guidelines for humane treatment did not exist at the time of the U.S.-Mexican War, but attacking civilians was considered an atrocity even at that time. It was not until the Geneva Convention of 1949 that an agreement about what constitutes inhuman treatment of civilians, prisoners, and other noncombatants in wartime was established.

bivouac   A temporary camp for army troops, usually in an unsheltered area.

blockade   Isolating a port, city, region, or nation by surrounding it with ships or troops to prevent the passage of traffic or supplies. To blockade an international boundary or a sovereign nation, as General Taylor blockaded the mouth of the Rio Grande on April 12, 1846, is considered a breach of international law and a hostile act inviting military response.

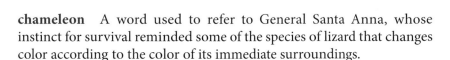

chameleon   A word used to refer to General Santa Anna, whose instinct for survival reminded some of the species of lizard that changes color according to the color of its immediate surroundings.

declaration of war   A vote in Congress is necessary for a war to be officially declared. The U.S.-Mexican War got such a vote but some American "wars"—in Vietnam, for example—did not and so are sometimes referred to as "conflicts."

deserters of conscience   In the U.S.-Mexican War, recruits who abandoned the U.S. Army to join the Mexican forces in protest against the atrocities committed against Catholic Mexicans and their places of worship. Many of these were Irish immigrants, who formed the San Patricio Brigade.

draft animals   Animals used to transport heavy loads, cannon, and supplies. In the U.S.-Mexican War, the draft animals of choice were mules, because they could negotiate the rough Mexican terrain and subsist on the local vegetation.

dragoon   A soldier who rode a horse into battle and, unlike traditional cavalry members, might dismount to engage in battle. Originally, dragoons were armed with swords, but in the war against Mexico the term also referred to mounted soldiers who bore rifles.

estadounidenses   Spanish for U.S. citizens or those from the United States. **Norteamericanos,** or people from North America, is similarly used.

expansionists   Believers in Manifest Destiny, the doctrine that the United States had a divine right to all the territories of North America. (See **Young America.**)

flogging   At the time of the U.S.-Mexican War, the use of a whip to punish the soldier for minor and major infractions of military law.

Freemason   Originally this referred to the independent or freelance stonemasons of medieval times. Since the 1700s, *Mason* refers to a member of a now international society with its own secret beliefs, rituals, symbols, and, most relevant here, with intense fraternal loyalties among its members. Although Texas's Gen. Sam Houston captured General Santa Anna, both were Masons, and Houston was bound to defend a brother Mason.

gringo   Mexican slang for "North American." One etymology traces it to the Spanish for "Greek," *Griego,* referring to an unknown or foreign person or language (as in the American idiom "It's all Greek to me.") Others claim it was coined at the time of the U.S.-Mexican War and was perhaps derived from a popular song sung by U.S. troops, "Green grow the rushes, oh."

Indian Removal   The policy of removing—driving out—Native Americans from their traditional homelands and forcing them to resettle in lands not wanted by white Americans at the time. Although it is a policy and practice particularly associated with Andrew Jackson, it was originally proposed by Thomas Jefferson and it continued to be enforced long after Jackson's term as president.

latitude   The imaginary parallel lines that divide up the surface of the Earth on the north-south axis. Latitude is measured in degrees north and south, each starting from the equator. In his 1844 campaign for president, Democrat James Polk used the slogan, "54-40 or Fight," a reference to the latitude that expansionists wanted as the northernmost border of the coveted Oregon Territory. In the end, President Polk had to settle for 49° north latitude as the northwest boundary with Canada.

mission   Relating to the organization of a settlement around a church, it generally refers to Spanish or Mexican Catholic missions in rural areas.

panhandle   A narrow strip of land projecting from a defined area. Both Texas and Florida have panhandles. The Florida Panhandle, which extends under the borders of Alabama and Georgia, remained a Spanish possession until 1821.

peso   The Spanish word for "weight," it was another name for silver Spanish pieces of eight, the official coin of colonial Mexico. It is still used as the name for the basic coinage in Mexico today. The peso was used as legal currency not only in Mexico but, until February 21, 1857, in the United States as well. The U.S. dollar began as a renamed peso.

phalanx   A line or array of battle with soldiers in a tight formation. In the ancient world, the troops had their shields joined and long spears overlapping. In 1838–42, a commentator wrote that a "phalanx when once broken became wholly helpless," as, in fact, Santa Anna's similarly organized troops did in several battles.

pommel   The upright, handlelike projection on a western saddle. Gen. Zachary Taylor was noted for hooking one leg around the pommel and directing his battles sitting in this position.

pulque   Mild, fermented juice of the maguey cactus, native to Mexico and often consumed in *pulquerias* (roughly speaking, "beer halls"). In Veracruz, Scott's General Order No. 20 shut them down.

ratify   To formally approve or sanction, used especially in reference to government representatives signing a treaty or such agreement.

siesta   Derived from the Spanish word for "sixth," it refers to the sixth hour after sunrise, or noon, midday. It refers to the midday nap favored by people who live in extremely hot climates.

slave state   A southern, slaveholding state or a new state entering the Union as a slaveholding state. Intensive cultivation of cotton and other crops exhausted land rather quickly; Southerners assumed that upon expanding into new territory, they could bring their slaves. Abolitionists and Northerners feared a slave-state majority in the legislature.

surf boats   Flat-bottomed boats about 40 feet by 12 feet, pointed at bow and stern and used for General Scott's amphibious landing of troops and weapons at Veracruz.

thumping majorities   Huge majorities in Congress who enthusiastically voted to pursue the war against Mexico.

tierra caliente   Spanish for "hot land," this was one of several terms referring to the "fever zone," the area of yellow fever, a frequently lethal, mosquito-borne illness that killed many during the U.S.-Mexican War. The fever zone tended to be in a low, humid area.

Yanqui   The Spanish phonetic spelling of "Yankee" or North American.

Young America   Related to the concept of Manifest Destiny, it differed to some degree in that it emphasized democratic progress and did not believe in the necessity of slavery in these newly acquired territories.

Further Reading

NONFICTION

Beauregard, P. G. T. *With Beauregard in Mexico: The Mexican War Reminiscences of P. T. G. Beauregard.* Edited by T. Harry Williams. New York: Da Capo Press, 1969.

Breithaupt, Richard. *The Aztec Club: Military Society of the Mexican War.* Universal City, Calif.: Walika Publishing, 1998.

Chalfant, William. *Dangerous Passage: The Santa Fe Trail and the Mexican War.* Norman: University of Oklahoma Press, 1994.

Christensen, Thomas. *The U.S.-Mexican War.* San Francisco: Bay Books, 1998.

Cress, Lawrence Delbert, ed. *Dispatches from the Mexican War.* Norman: University of Oklahoma Press, 1999.

Crawford, Anna Fears, ed. *The Eagle: The Autobiography of Santa Anna.* Austin, Tex.: Pemberton Press, 1967.

Crutchfield, James Andrew. *Tragedy at Taos: The Revolt of 1847.* Plano, Tex.: Republic of Texas Press, 1995.

Davis, William C. *Three Roads to the Alamo: The Lives and Fortunes of David Crockett, James Bowie, and William Barret Travis.* New York: HarperCollins, 1999.

Dawson, Joseph G., III. *Doniphan's Epic March.* Louisville: University Press of Kentucky, 1999.

De La Peña, José Enrique. *With Santa Anna in Texas: A Personal Narrative of the Revolution.* College Station: Texas A&M University Press, 1997.

Drumm, Madeleine, ed. *Down the Santa Fe Trail and into Mexico: The Diary of Susan Shelby Magoffin, 1846–1847.* Lincoln: University of Nebraska Press, 1984.

Eisenhower, John S. D. *So Far from God: The U.S. War with Mexico 1846–1848.* New York: Doubleday, 1989.

Ferrell, Robert H., ed. *Monterrey Is Ours!: The Mexican War Letters of Lieutenant Dana, 1845–1847.* Louisville: University Press of Kentucky, 1990.

Field, Ron. *History of Uniforms: Mexican-American War 1846–1848.* Color plates by Richard Hook. London, England: Brassey's, 1997.

Frémont, John Charles. *Memoirs of My Life: Including Three Journeys of Western Exploration During the Years 1842, 1843–1844, 1845–1847.* New York: Cooper Square Press, 2001.

Gibson, George Rutledge. *Over the Chihuahua and Santa Fe Trails, 1847–1848: George Rutledge Gibson's Journal.* Edited by Robert W. Frazer. Albuquerque: University of New Mexico Press, 1981.

Hogan, Michael. *The Irish Soldiers of Mexico.* Guadalajara, Mexico: Fondo Editorial Universitario, 1998.

Johannsen, Robert W. *To the Halls of the Montezumas: The Mexican War in the American Imagination.* New York: Oxford University Press, 1985.

Lavendar, David Sievert. *Bent's Fort.* Lincoln: University of Nebraska Press, 1972.

Mahin, Dean B. *Olive Branch and Sword: The United States and Mexico, 1845–1848.* Jefferson, N.C.: McFarland, 1997.

McCaffrey, James M. *Army of Manifest Destiny: The American Soldier in the Mexican War, 1846–1848.* New York: New York University Press, 1992.

———. ed. *Surrounded by Dangers of All Kinds: The Mexican War Letters of Lieutenant Theodore Laidley.* Denton: University of North Texas Press, 1997.

Miller, Robert Ryal. *Shamrock and Sword: The Saint Patrick's Battalion in the U.S.-Mexican War.* Norman: University of Oklahoma Press, 1997.

Nardo, Don. *The Mexican-American War.* San Diego, Calif.: Lucent Books, 1999.

Ohrt, Wallace. *Defiant Peacemaker: Nicholas Trist in the Mexican War.* College Station: Texas A&M University Press, 1998.

Paz, Octavio. *The Labyrinth of Solitude.* Translated by Lysander Kemp. New York: Grove Press, 1985.

Robinson, Cecil, ed. *The View from Chapultepec: Mexican Writers on the Mexican-American War.* Tucson: University of Arizona Press, 1989.

Smith, George Winston. *Chronicles of the Gringos: the U.S. Army in the Mexican War, 1846–1848.* Albuquerque: University of New Mexico Press, 1968.

Smith, Gustavus Woodson. "Company 'A' Corps of Engineers, U.S.A. 1846–1848," in *The Mexican War by Gustavus Woodson Smith.* Edited by Leonne M. Hudson. Kent, Ohio: Kent State University Press, 2001.

Stevens, Peter F. *The Rogue's March: John Riley and the St. Patrick's Battalion, 1846–48.* London: Brassey's, 1999

Walker, Dale L. *Bear Flag Rising: The Conquest of California, 1846.* New York: Forge Books, 2000.

Webster, Frances Marvin Smith. *The Websters: Letters of an American Army Family in Peace and War, 1836–1853.* Edited by Van R. Baker. Kent, Ohio: Kent State University Press, 2000.

Wheelan, Joseph. *Invading Mexico: America's Continental Dream and the Mexican War, 1846–1848.* New York: Carroll & Graf, 2007.

Winders, Richard. *Mr. Polk's Army: American Military Experience in the Mexican War.* College Station: Texas A&M University Press, 1997.

Zeh, Frederick. *An Immigrant Soldier in the Mexican War.* Edited and translated by William J. Orr. College Station: Texas A&M University Press, 1995.

FICTION

Anaya, Rodolfo. *Bless Me, Ultima.* New York: Prentice Hall, 1995.

Azuela, Mariano. *The Underdogs: A Novel of the Mexican Revolution.* Translated by E. Munguia. New York: Signet, 1996.

Cather, Willa. *Death Comes for the Archbishop.* New York: Vintage Books, 1990.

Cutler, Bruce. *At War with Mexico: A Fictional Mosaic of the Times.* Literature of the American West Series, vol. 6. Tulsa: University of Oklahoma Press, 2001.

Dobie, J. Frank. "The Battlefields of Palo Alto and Resaca de La Palma" in *Legends of Texas: Lost Mines and Buried Treasure.* Gretna, La.: Pelican Pub. Co., 1992.

Fuentes, Carlos. *Burnt Water.* Translated by Margaret Sayers Peden. New York: Noonday Press, 1980.

Harrington, Stephen. *The Gates of the Alamo.* New York: Knopf, 2001.

Lowell, James Russell. *The Biglow Papers.* Edited by Homer Wilbur. St. Clair Shores, Mich.: Scholarly Press, 1971.

Michener, James. *Mexico.* New York: Random House, 1992.

Rulfo, Juan. *Pedro Páramo.* Translated by Margaret Sayers Peden. New York: Grove Press, 1994.

Shaara, Jeff M. *Gone for Soldiers: A Novel of the Mexican War.* New York: Ballantine Books, 2000.

Zollinger, Norman. *Meridian.* New York: Forge Books, 2000.

WEB SITES

Arnold, Linda. *The Mexican-American War and the Media, 1845–1848.* Available online. URL: http://www.history.vt.edu/MxAmWar/INDEX.html.

Blanding, Doreen. *Mexican American War: Blood for Land.* Available online. URL: http://www.waldsfe.org/UnitStudies/mexamerican.htm.

Descendants of Mexican War Veterans, The. *The U.S.-Mexican War, 1846–1848.* Available online. URL: http://www.dmwv.org/mexwar/mexwar1.htm.

The History Guy: The U.S.-Mexican War (1846–1848). Available online. URL: http://www.historyguy.com/Mexican-American_War.html.

The Mexican War. Available online. URL: http://www.latinamericanstudies.org/mexican.html.

Public Broadcasting Service. *U.S.-Mexican War, 1846–1848.* Available online. URL: http://www.pbs.org/kera/usmexicanwar.

Index

Page numbers in *italic* indicate a photograph. Page numbers followed by *m* indicate maps. Page numbers followed by *g* indicate glossary entries. Page numbers in **boldface** indicate box features.